CAMBRIDGE LIBRARY COLLECTION

Books of enduring scholarly value

Egyptology

The large-scale scientific investigation of Egyptian antiquities by Western scholars began as an unintended consequence of Napoleon's invasion of Egypt during which, in 1799, the Rosetta Stone was discovered. The military expedition was accompanied by French scholars, whose reports prompted a wave of enthusiasm that swept across Europe and North America resulting in the Egyptian Revival style in art and architecture. Increasing numbers of tourists visited Egypt, eager to see the marvels being revealed by archaeological excavation. Writers and booksellers responded to this growing interest with publications ranging from technical site reports to tourist guidebooks and from children's histories to theories identifying the pyramids as repositories of esoteric knowledge. This series reissues a wide selection of such books. They reveal the gradual change from the 'tomb-robbing' approach of early excavators to the highly organised and systematic approach of Flinders Petrie, the 'father of Egyptology', and include early accounts of the decipherment of the hieroglyphic script.

Abydos

Originally published between 1902 and 1904 for the Egypt Exploration Fund, this three-volume set of reports documents the excavations begun by the pioneering archaeologist Sir William Matthew Flinders Petrie (1853–1942) at one of ancient Egypt's most sacred sites, the necropolis at Abydos. These reports follow on from the findings that Petrie published in *The Royal Tombs of the First Dynasty* (1900) and *The Royal Tombs of the Earliest Dynasties* (1901), both of which are reissued in this series. Volume 3 was produced by Petrie's younger colleagues, Edward Russell Ayrton (1882–1914), Charles Trick Currelly (1876–1956) and Arthur Weigall (1880–1934). The report includes chapters on the tombs of Senusret III and Ahmose I. More than sixty pages of plates illustrate the discoveries, which range from simple flint implements to elaborate stelae. A chapter by Alan Gardiner (1879–1963) sheds light on the inscriptions.

T0371122

Abydos

Volume 3

Edward Russell Ayrton
C.T. Currelly
A.E. Weigall

CAMBRIDGE
UNIVERSITY PRESS

CAMBRIDGE
UNIVERSITY PRESS

University Printing House, Cambridge, CB2 8BS, United Kingdom

Published in the United States of America by Cambridge University Press, New York

Cambridge University Press is part of the University of Cambridge.
It furthers the University's mission by disseminating knowledge in the pursuit of
education, learning and research at the highest international levels of excellence.

www.cambridge.org
Information on this title: www.cambridge.org/9781108068406

© in this compilation Cambridge University Press 2013

This edition first published 1904
This digitally printed version 2013

ISBN 978-1-108-06840-6 Paperback

ABYDOS

PART III.   1904

BY

E. R. AYRTON, C. T. CURRELLY, M.A., AND A. E. P. WEIGALL

With a Chapter by

A. H. GARDINER, B.A.

SPECIAL EXTRA PUBLICATION OF

THE EGYPT EXPLORATION FUND

PUBLISHED BY ORDER OF THE COMMITTEE

LONDON

SOLD AT

THE OFFICES OF THE EGYPT EXPLORATION FUND, 37, GREAT RUSSELL STREET, W.C.

AND 8, BEACON STREET, BOSTON, MASS., U.S.A.

AND BY KEGAN PAUL, TRENCH, TRÜBNER & CO., DRYDEN HOUSE, 43, GERRARD STREET, SOHO, W.

B. QUARITCH, 15, PICCADILLY, W.; ASHER & CO., 13, BEDFORD STREET, COVENT GARDEN, W.C.

AND HENRY FROWDE, AMEN CORNER, E.C.

—

1904

LONDON:
PRINTED BY GILBERT AND RIVINGTON LIMITED,
ST. JOHN'S HOUSE, CLERKENWELL.

EGYPT EXPLORATION FUND.

[The reading of Senusert for Usertesen having been now proved by a contemporary spelling, this form is adopted here.]

CONTENTS OF PART III.

——•◦•——

CHAPTER V.

THE TOMB OF AAHMES I
(C. T. CURRELLY).

CHAPTER VI.

THE SHRINE OF TETA-SHERA
(C. T. CURRELLY).

CHAPTER VII.

THE INSCRIPTIONS
(A. H. GARDINER).

CHAPTER VIII.

DESCRIPTION OF PLATES.

LIST OF PLATES

WITH REFERENCES TO THE PAGES ON WHICH THEY ARE DESCRIBED.

————••————

* See Note above Contents.

ABYDOS III.

CHAPTER I.

THE SHUNEH, MIDDLE FORT AND DEIR.

By E. R. Ayrton.

1. THE great cemetery of Abydos is divided into two parts by the valley which runs up to the Royal Tombs. In the midst of the northern part stands a high fortress of brickwork, the dark mass of which is the most prominent feature of Abydos. Although a well-known place, yet its real nature had still to be worked out, and the excavation of it occupied most of my time this season. To the modern Egyptian this building is known as the "Shunet-ez-Zebib" or "storehouse of dried grapes," which Roche-monteix suggests is probably a corruption of the ancient name [hieroglyphs] (or [hieroglyphs]) [hieroglyphs], "The place of the ibis-vases," (*Œuvres diverses*, Num. § iii, p. 80.), because, from the XXIInd Dynasty onward, the greater part of the enclosure was used as a cemetery for the sacred birds.

Nearly the whole of the eastern half of the Shuneh was dug over by Mariette's workmen, and a general plan and section were made at the same time (MARIETTE, *Abydos* II, p. 46 and pl. 68). Nothing seems to have been found without the actual enclosure of the fort, except a very large number of vases containing the mummied ibis, some of which had brightly-coloured scenes upon them and a dedication to Thoth of Hermopolis.

In the narrow space which separates the two walls, nothing was then found on the north, east, or west sides. But the space on the south side seems to have been used as a cemetery; there the walls were hollowed out in parts, and small coffins of coarse baked clay, containing infants, were placed in the recesses. Steles upon which were the invocations to [hieroglyphs] "Osiris, lord of birth," were also placed in the walls. These coffins and steles were of course later than the XIXth Dynasty. Mariette, however, found no object which could throw any light on the date of building of the fort. M. Maspero at first considered that it was built towards the time of the XVIIIth Dynasty, but changed his opinion in favour of the period between the VIth and XIIth Dynasties (*Dawn of Civilization*, p. 450, note 5), basing his argument entirely on the style of building. Within the enclosure of the Shuneh are a series of chambers, built rather askew to the other walls, with an entrance in the north face. Mariette notices the most southern of these on his plan, but considers their building to have been later than that of the rest of the fort.

2. Before I arrived on the scene of the excavations, Mr. Currelly, who was engaged on some cemetery work to the west of the Shuneh,

discovered there what seemed to be two long parallel walls running N.W. and S.E.; and, afterwards when the digging in the Shuneh was nearly at an end, some of the men were turned on to dig trenches in this region, and search for anything which might help us to find a clue. These thin lines of brick were only some six inches high, owing to the excessive denudation which they had sustained from wind and sand. But we soon found a connecting wall to the south, and saw that we were digging in an immense enclosure. On running trenches across we found a small building near the south-east corner, which bore a great resemblance to a small mastaba chapel. However, although we cleared away the loose sand all around, we found no tomb-shaft; and came to the conclusion from the objects found in it that this must be an Old Kingdom house within a court or fortification. This building and court will be called the "Middle Fort" throughout the present volume.

3. The reason for the use of the term "Middle Fort" will become apparent on turning to the sketch map on pl. viii, which roughly indicates the ground covered by the excavations. It will also be noticed from this that there is another large building to the north of the Shuneh with an entrance on the east side. This building, known as the Coptic Deir, has unfortunately been used as a home by the Copts of the neighbourhood for a long time past, and is now completely filled up by a flourishing little village and church. From the general plan and style of building this enclosure seems to belong to the same period as the Shuneh Fort, and should we ever be able to excavate it, we might probably find in the interior a small building similar to those in the Shuneh and Middle Fort.

We have here therefore three great buildings, probably all for the same purpose and of approximately the same age.

4. On looking at the plans of the two enclosures which we were able to examine, it will at once be noticed that the same plan and style of ornamentation was followed in both cases. On the west we have a long wall with single pilasters averaging 21 in. broad, with a space of from 22-24 in. between. The small narrow entrance on the west which leads into the interior of the Shuneh is, however, omitted in the Middle Fort, though it is quite possible that it existed further to the north where the wall has been destroyed. On the south we have a similar row of single pilasters, and in both cases a narrow entrance leads into the interior, closed originally by a wooden door opening outwards. To the east the wall, as is the case in tombs or mastabas, is more complicated in its design. That of the Shuneh is composed of groups of four pilasters similar in breadth and depth to those on the south and west walls; but between these groups the wall recedes to double the depth of an ordinary pilaster, forming a deep recess, resembling the false door found in mastabas and tomb chapels, and then usually only on the east wall. Here, however, the proportion of depth to width is greater than is found in the mastaba. The east wall of the Middle Fort is similar in design, with the exception that the deeper recesses separate groups of five instead of four pilasters.

In the south-east corner of each fort is an entrance leading into a small court and thence to the interior. It is worth noting that in each case the real doors differ in plan but little from the false. In fact a false door continued inwards and widened slightly would serve equally well as an entrance.

5. That the use of pilasters to decorate the outer side of a wall is as old as the Ist Dynasty, we see from the tomb of Mena, excavated at Negadeh by M. de Morgan; where a much more elaborate type of building was followed than in the Shuneh.

6. The walls of both the Shuneh and Middle Fort were coated on both the inner and

outer sides with a plaster of mud, some ¾ in. thick, on which was a thin layer of white plaster or stucco. This was left plain in the case of the Shuneh; but around the walls of the Middle Fort was painted a strip of dark red, 4 ins. broad at a height of 22 ins. above the ground. The interior of the small court of the S.E. gate was similarly painted, with a band 3½ ins. broad. The great wall of the Shuneh at present reaches a height of some 36 ft. and originally may even have reached 40 ft. Its average breadth at the bottom is 210 in., with a slight batter which would make the breadth at the top about 180 in. The small surrounding wall reaches a height of 18—20 ft. at its highest point on the north, and the original height was probably not much more; its width varies from 6 to 8 ft. Nothing was discovered which could show by what method access was obtained to the top of the walls, but this may have been by wooden ladders; although it seems improbable that there were ever any hollows in the walls in which to place them, as has been suggested. The wall of the older fort to the north was at one time at least 15 ft. high; its breadth at present is 4 ft. Of the original height of the chambers in either of the forts nothing can be said, since only about 4 ft. of brickwork remains above the foundations. The walls of both forts are founded in trenches only about 6 in. below the original desert surface.

Unfortunately, owing to the presence of the modern cemetery of the Copts, we could not excavate the north wall of the Middle Fort; but if it at all resembled that of the Shuneh there was probably another elaborate entrance in the N.E. corner.

The outside of the Coptic Deir is unfortunately too much weathered to show whether the decoration on the walls resembled that on the Shuneh or Middle Fort. And at present the only entrance is that to the north, though there may possibly have been gates on the other three sides; since great gaps are now visible, though filled with rubbish.

7. The chambers discovered in the Shuneh and Middle Fort do not agree in detail. Those in the Shuneh have pilasters along the west wall and entrance on the east, with pilasters and one false door in the middle. The north wall was plain and the south wall was too broken to show any face. There was a coating of stucco both inside and out, of the same material as that on the great walls.

The small chambers in the Middle Fort have two plain walls; but the wall to the east is beautifully decorated with a series of recesses, the entrance being in the S.E. corner. The eastern part of the southern wall, which was also visible from the gate, was decorated with single pilasters, while the western part was left plain. These chambers were also decorated inside and out with white stucco.

Various objects were found which enable us to ascertain the date of the building of the Shuneh. A sealing of Khasekhemui, fifth (?) king of the IInd Dynasty, was found in the eastern portion of room F, at a height of 6 in. from the floor, where it had probably been thrown at a later period. The base of a IInd Dynasty vase, similar to No. 28 (pl. xxxii), was found at G, with another piece of a sealing of Khasekhemui. There are no traces of any earlier objects, and we may thus consider that this house was built during the reign of king Khasekhemui. Sealings, which from their style appear to belong to the IIIrd—IVth Dynasties, were found near the entrance, at A. The lower part of a large VIth Dynasty jar was found at F. From these it seems probable that the chambers were in use down to the VIth Dynasty. The chamber G was filled with feathers and charred remains of the sacred ibis; and chambers J and B had been bricked up and re-used as store-chambers in later times, since 6 in. of sand had accumulated on the floors.

8. On the plan, at 153 in. to the west of the east wall, will be noticed a long narrow trench in the sand. At one time this probably held the foundations of a wall. Mariette on his plan notes the existence of a wall running west from the east wall in the south-east corner, and then north, as though to join a wall built in this position; but of this no trace could be found. In the eastern corner the wall was found to have been built on the top of a thickness of 20 in. of brick rubbish, ox bones, and pots of the rough hand-made type, which is known from the end of the Ist to the IVth Dynasties (pl. xxxii, 1—4). Evidently the builders on coming to a hollow in the ground, filled it to the required level with the nearest rubbish, making use of even their own food vessels.

When the building of the Shuneh was begun, the Middle Fort was evidently considered inadequate for the purpose of defence, and consequently the Shuneh was built on a larger and more imposing scale. The Middle Fort was probably no longer a royal dwelling, as no care was taken to avoid interfering with the entrances.

9. The western trench of the Shuneh was half full of rubbish in Ramesside times, since many small bronze figures of Osiris belonging to that period were found at the depth of $\frac{3}{4}$ metre from the firm floor. A very fine pot of the Coptic period, ornamented with hunting scenes in yellow and black on a polished red surface, similar to the designs on the textiles, was found $\frac{1}{2}$ metre higher. The fort itself, or at least the northern portion, had fallen into disuse before the XIIth Dynasty, because in the N.W. corner a great drift of sand reaches to a height of 4 metres, and in this, at 2 metres from the ground, was found a child's burial of the XIIth Dynasty. A burial of the same date was found in an almost similar position in the rubbish of the north trench.

In the walls of the fort which were most sheltered from the cold winds the Copts had dug out hollows, and lining them with stucco had turned them into small rooms. In fact, the western wall is so honeycombed on the outer side in this way that it is marvellous it should have stood so long; the inner side of the eastern wall had been similarly weakened, but did not stand the test, and only some 12 ft. of wall remain (cf. photograph, pl. v). The Shuneh, then, narrowly escaped being turned into a Coptic village like the Deir; and it seems probable that, had it not been for the Copts, the four walls would still be standing as they were built.

10. The dating of the Middle Fort is also given by sealings. At A was found a very fine sealing of Perabsen, fourth king of the IInd Dynasty (pl. ix, No. 3), besides two scraps (Nos. 1 and 2), similar to some found at the Royal Tombs (*R.T.* i, 184-5); together with other sealings which from their style appear to belong to the same date. A fine sealing of Khasekhemui was found at B, and several sealings were discovered in the court of the gate. In room K was found the pottery marked μ 46 on pl. xxxii: a fine IInd Dynasty jar of whitened pottery with dishes of the same date.

The Middle Fort was therefore older than the Shuneh, as it contains the earlier sealings, those of Perabsen. That it had fallen into disuse by the beginning of the VIth Dynasty is shown by the number of burials of that date in the courtyard.

It is probable, then, that here are a series of royal forts built in the IInd Dynasty, which served as residences for the kings when they came to worship at the temple of Abydos, which stood between these buildings and the cultivated land. (Gen. plan, pl. v.)

11. The fort at Hierakonpolis, although smaller, is similar to the Shuneh in most respects. (Cf. QUIBELL, *Hierakonpolis II*, pp. 19 and 20, and pl. lxxiv.) There are two

walls, a large enclosure-wall and a small surrounding one. As in the Shuneh the greater wall is ornamented with panelling, though evidently without any trace of false doors on the eastern wall. Only one entrance remains; it is situated in the east corner, and seems to be similar in pattern to the corresponding gateway in the Shuneh, except that here, owing to the comparative thinness of the wall, the court has been built out in a block of building. The walls are of unbaked brick covered with a mud plastering, the surface of which is whitened. The pilasters in width and depth seem to correspond with those of the Shuneh.

The great wall has a thickness of 180 in. and the smaller one of 72 in. No openings, however, were found in the Shuneh like those on each side of this gateway. Unfortunately no objects were found which could help to date this fort except some Old Kingdom pottery, though to what portion of the Old Kingdom this pottery is dated Mr. Quibell does not state. He also mentions that some archaic graves were found under the wall. The resemblance between the fort at Hierakonpolis and the Shuneh and Middle Fort at Abydos is certainly striking, both in architecture and situation. They are situated to the west of the large temple sites of Hierakonpolis and Abydos respectively, where temples have existed from at least the Ist Dynasty.

12. Maspero has pointed out that the hieroglyph ⌷ is probably derived from large buildings, such as the Shuneh, and that the small rectangle in the corner perhaps corresponds to an elaborate gateway such as the northern entrance of the Shuneh fort. (Cf. *P.S.B.A.*, 1889-90, p. 247; *R.T.* ii, xii, 3.)

The Middle Fort was used in later times as a cemetery and a few burials were found in the Shuneh. These will be mentioned in the description of the plates (chap. ii).

CHAPTER II.

THE CEMETERY.

By C. T. Currelly, M.A.

13. THE excavations described in this chapter were begun in the fringe of the cemetery on the southern slope of the valley leading to the Royal Tombs. A small part of this area, descending from the cemetery to the valley, had not been touched by any previous explorer, and we were anxious to find out if the tombs extended right down to the valley.

A series of trenches was started from the floor of the valley, and the men, working in parallel lines, gradually advanced up the slope. Each pair of men dug down through the wind-blown sand to that deposited by water action. They can easily tell when this latter is reached, for by constant friction the drifting sands acquire considerable polish. When once this under-crust of water-laid sand is reached an experienced digger can usually determine whether it is untouched or has been dug through before.

14. The first bodies found were merely skeletons, with nothing to afford evidence of their date. Many others were merely piles of bones, buried loosely in the sand, or in some cases enclosed in a small box into which they had been heaped. These were no doubt remains which had been brought from considerable distances, in order that the departed might have the benefits derived from the great sanctity of the site, and also to be at the place of departure when the souls started for the mystic land of the west.

Some had evidently been soldiers killed on distant campaigns, whose bones had been brought here to be near the sanctuary. One skull in particular showed how a man could be hacked to pieces by sharp weapons. He had first received two terrible cuts on the back of the head; then while he was throwing back his head to escape another blow, his opponent's blade must have caught the point of the chin, completing severing the two sides of the lower jaw. Probably now no longer able to keep up his guard, he received a sweeping blow that cut a slice off the skull over the right temple and exposed the brain. White ants had reduced the coffin to powder, but a few scraps of stucco showed that it was of about the XXVIth Dynasty, the time of the Persian wars.

As we descended the hill the tombs were closer together, and were mostly of the XIth Dynasty. One burial, quite definitely of this period, was contracted, the body lying facing the east, with the head to the north, and the knees drawn up. The other tombs yielded nothing and were not of any particular interest in their construction.

15. At the close of the first day's work, one of the men came to say he had found a box. I at once went with him to his pit, and perceived that he had put his *turiyeh* through the sides of what had once been a box, before the white ants had reduced the wood to powder. Where his flat pick had gone in a small bronze statuette could be seen. Very carefully we removed the sand all around, and soon found a mass of bronzes, of different sizes and designs, about six hundred in number, all votive offerings of the XXVIth Dynasty. The greater number

were statuettes of Osiris, either standing or seated, but several were of Isis and Horus, and there were also a few crowned serpents, small plumes, and even scraps of bronze. Several of the larger figures were broken, revealing the way in which they had been made. An ash core was moulded as nearly as possible to the form intended for the statuette. Sometimes this core was stiffened by having in its centre a splinter of wood. This ash statuette was then dipped lightly in melted wax and the thin layer that adhered was modelled by the artist in order to make certain parts sharper. Round this the mould was packed, and then the whole mass was heated, and the wax as it melted soaked into the mould. This done the metal could be poured in, so as to form a cast almost as thin as paper. An English sculptor, who examined them carefully, said he did not believe any casting could be done in England that would be as thin and at the same time give the same sharpness.

Naturally the question arose, why the box had been buried there. As temples must continually have become crowded with votive offerings, no doubt such things were removed at regular intervals. Probably having been once dedicated to the deity, the images acquired a sacredness which saved them from the melting-pot, or from being removed to another part of the country and sold to new worshippers. This would have seemed quite definite but for the waste pieces and some figures that, having been spoilt evidently in the casting, could never have been sold or dedicated. If this were a trader's box the scraps would be accounted for from the value of the metal. But were votive offerings ever in traders' hands? Certainly this is not the custom with such things to-day. And also why should they be buried in a cemetery at that distance from the town? What seems to me most probable is that the whole manufacture and sale of votive offerings was in the hands of the priesthood. Possibly it was an important source of revenue for the temple. If so it can easily be imagined that the sacredness would gradually widen. Beginning with an image sacred only when dedicated to the god, after a little every thing used in the making of the image would be sacred, so that dedicated or not, any metal that had taken the image of the god, no matter how imperfectly, would acquire a mystic nature, and therefore would not be re-used.

16. As two days were quite sufficient to work over this small part of the slope, and this was only preliminary work while the men were being assembled and organized, we went on the morning of the third day to the Shuneh, and the cemetery north and west from there.

This cemetery has been plundered for the last thirty years and more. The first excavation was by Mariette's overseers, who dug for thirteen years, in one part or another; long afterwards the *Mission Amélineau* worked over what was left. So now we came to it, knowing that our chief chance of obtaining unopened tombs, that would yield information and antiquities, lay in the extraordinary skill of our Qufti workmen. These men have been with Professor Petrie for eleven years, and thanks to his system of digging and to the immense amount of personal attention, they are now probably the best excavators in the world. As this was also a preliminary piece of work, the tombs are only described for their more important contents.

At first the men started to probe for tombs directly north of the Shuneh; here were numerous small mastabas, cut down by sand action to a level with the ground. Here and there among them, without any order, were pit tombs. The only one of any importance had the chambers both north and south of the shaft—see pl. xx. In the south chamber there was a contracted burial, with a string of small green beads of the XIth Dynasty, wound three times round the wrist.

During the first day's search two of the men

came on a very long wall, buried a few inches below the surface, and shortly after a wall was found parallel to it and at some distance; this was left to be worked carefully by Mr. Ayrton, who has described it under the name of the Middle Fort in the preceding chapter.

17. Gradually the men worked westwards, sinking small pits at every few feet. These either reached down to untouched *gebel*, that is, water-deposited sand, or else to indications of a tomb, shown by a hole having been dug in the *gebel*, or by actual brickwork. At times to find the *gebel* it only needed a few scrapes with the pick; at other times it was necessary to dig down through two or three feet of accumulated rubbish and wind-drifted sand.

The great bulk of the tombs which had escaped recent search had been plundered anciently: it was therefore impossible in most cases to say what had been placed with the bodies, or even what had been the original position of the bodies in the tomb. We found many cases where from six to twelve bodies had been buried at different times in one tomb; and in such tombs most of the bones had been pushed aside into a heap to make room for the next body, and so anything that had been overlooked by the plunderers was in no relation to the body with which it had been buried.

18. One tomb, ν 21, pl. xx, had a deep pit, with one chamber near the surface and another lower down. Both had been plundered anciently. Fortunately for us there was also a third chamber considerably below these. Much of the gravel forming the roof of this chamber had fallen in and broken up the burials, the whole contents of the chamber was therefore worked over with a sieve. Owing to this all the relative positions were lost, and the objects only were rescued. It was a rich burial of the XIIth Dynasty, with two bodies side by side. It took about half a day to sift and re-sift the accumulated sand and gravel. Four of the Quftis, with their faces beaming with excite-

ment, shook the fine sand through the sieve, and picked from it the beads and amulets in gold, electrum, silver, lazuli, carnelian, amethyst, and green felspar; and the so-called blue marble kohl-pots and dishes. By far the most beautiful object was a group of small carnelian and green felspar beads. This had been a necklace of three strings, held together at intervals by silver claws (pl. xii). These, as well as the other necklaces and amulets, were of exquisite workmanship and of great beauty of form. Another group of very fine and delicate gold amulets is shown on pl. xii. The first line has kneeling figures holding palm branches, the emblems of eternity; the second line has, first, the standing jackal, Upuaut, next come two jackals lying on pedestals, with their tails hanging down, and then another Upuaut. Below this is a very small image of Min, with his raised hand holding the flail.

It is interesting to notice in this small group of amulets, the prominence given to the gods of life and death, especially the latter. Min is the god who gives life, the one who produces from the field and herds, the earth-god of reproduction. Under one form or another he seems to have been worshipped all round the Mediterranean. The association of the jackal with death shows a god of a different kind, who is found in a much more limited area. Instead of a great power of nature being deified, the worship of the jackal comes entirely from an association of ideas. The jackal living in the desert for generations, knows all its slopes and valleys, and lucky is it for the desert traveller who finds a lonely jackal track. In this way the jackal becomes the symbol of a guide through the unknown. To transfer the idea from the desert journey to the blessed west, passing through the shadowy regions of the after-life, and to deify the standing jackal, Upuaut, is a natural connection of thought. In this way Upuaut became the early god of

Abydos, the place from which he leads the souls of the departed to the mysterious land of the west.

The jackal on the pedestal, Anubis, is the one that prowls through the cemeteries at night, eating the offerings from the tombs, and thus becomes associated with the dead, and later with the embalmed body and the processes of embalming.

The workmanship of these amulets is excellent. Gold, electrum, and silver are used with great skill; the cutting of the stone also shows considerable ability, but hardly up to the standard of the metal work. The two scarabs are green felspar with silver setting.

19. The other tomb of particular interest is of the XXth Dynasty. It was vaulted and decorated with scenes and inscriptions, see pls. xxvi–xxviii. Over the mud plaster a thin coat of white stucco had been laid, and the decoration painted in black and red.

The chief scene is on the wall opposite the entrance (see pl. xxviii). The deceased, Hor-dedu-ankh, is standing before Osiris. The great god is seated on his throne. At his feet springs up the lotus, on which are the sons of Horus, the four genii of the dead. Behind him is his sister-wife, Isis, with her hand raised; and above all comes the red sun, in the boat on which it floats along the celestial Nile.

Round the small entrance arch is the drawing at the top of pl. xxvi. Here is the winged beetle with the emblem of the rising sun which it rolls round its daily course; and below this, the sacred cow of Isis on the left, and on the right two of her girdle ties, and the emblem of stability, the *dad*. At the bottom on either side are the keepers of the gate, with the great knife drawn.

The second scene shows the shrine of Osiris with two drawings of the deceased, one on either side, in the attitude of supplication. The one on the right has before him a table of offerings across which has been placed the lotus. Within the shrine is seated Osiris, with the lotus and the genii of the dead. Behind him are his sister-wife Isis and his sister Nephthys (Nebhat), and before him his son Horus. Behind the figure of the deceased, standing on the left side of the drawing, come the long lines of the Negative Confession from the *Book of the Dead*, see plate xxvii.

On the west wall were two drawings. The smaller one seems to represent the boat of the sun being drawn along, and behind it a sort of barge on which a number of gods are seated. Behind this the deceased is kneeling for admission.

The scene below was farther along the same wall and represents the judgment. The deceased stands watching the weighing of his heart, Anubis has placed it in the left pan of the balance, and in the right pan he has placed Maat, the goddess of Truth and Justice. Sin is heavy; should the heart sink, it is immediately thrown to the devourer of hearts waiting at the foot of the scales, the monster Amemt. To the right stands Thoth ready to record for Osiris the judgment.

Lastly, overhead extended the outstretched figure of Nut, and just where the spring of the arch started came two twisting serpents with their mouths open.

The drawing of the figures is very conventional, a result of carelessness and repeated copying. The brickwork on the other hand showed better workmanship; the arch of the roof is particularly good.

Against the west wall lay the skeleton at full length, one shoulder against the wall, the other resting on the ground. By the head were two pots. Beside it lay another body with a pile of beads where the head should have been. The bones of both skeletons had been disturbed to some extent and it was evident the tomb had been plundered. The plunderer had thrown some of the things up to the surface, where one of the strings of beads, having been lost in the sand, remained till we found it.

20. For some time I had noticed a large stone about half-a-mile further out on the desert. One day a couple of men were told off to sink a pit there, and on removing a few baskets-full of sand, found a large pile of stone chippings, mostly of fine limestone, but with some chips of brown sandstone. About three feet down we came on cut stones lying in position, and gradually removing the top rubbish, disclosed the foundations of a tomb-chapel. Near the big stone that had attracted my attention, the stele was found, see plate xiv. The chapel had been taken to pieces at a late period for building-stone, and the blocks re-cut on the spot. The stele shows the man for whom the chapel was built, Ay and his family, and the style places it definitely in the Middle Kingdom. The building was square and was truly oriented, while all the other tombs at Abydos conform to the diagonal line of the river.

In searching for the tomb pit we were unsuccessful. Trenches and pits were dug at a distance of two or three feet apart over a considerable area, but there was no sign of the *gebel* having been disturbed. Once we thought we had discovered it, and dug out a large hole, only to find that it was the rubbish hole for the broken bricks used in connection with the building.

A short distance away in the valley leading to the Royal Tombs there had been a building of some kind, and between this and the tomb-chapel of Ay a line of stones showed an ancient road. This was dug over by Mariette (*Abydos* II, 34), and he proved that it was built in the forty-second year of the reign of Rameses II. It is most probable the blocks taken from the chapel of Ay were drawn across to the Ramesside building.

Just as this excavation was finished many of the men must have received alarming messages from Quft, for the number who came with sad faces to say they were summoned home to see sick wives, so lessened our workers that we had to close the work, and let the remainder go a day before the commencement of the Bayram festivities, from which they returned a week later.

CHAPTER III.

TOMB AND CEMETERY OF SENUSERT III.

By Arthur E. P. Weigall.

21. The royal burial ground of the XIIth Dynasty known as Cemetery S is situated at the foot of the cliffs, about a mile south of the Royal Tombs and about the same distance south-west of the Temple of the Kings (Seti I). It lies in the shadow of the promontory which forms the southern extremity of the great desert bay of Abydos. At this point the limestone cliffs shelve down to the desert level in a series of terraces, covered with large boulders and loose stones, detached probably in Palaeolithic times from the summit. From the foot of the rocks extends a bed of blown sand about three feet deep over the whole site, some fourteen inches of which appear to have settled since the cemetery was constructed. Below this there are the more compact gravel and sand deposits, which continue down to the underlying rocks at a depth ranging from a foot to forty feet in the excavated area. The whole desert surface slopes gently towards the arable land, which lies about half-a-mile away, being some nine miles from the Nile.

The site was first observed by M. Amélineau during his residence at Abydos, but no real excavations were carried on by him here. He attempted, however, to clear one of the large tombs (S 9), his endeavours being frustrated by the fact that the sand immediately ran in on the parts laid bare by his men—a not unprecedented occurrence at the outset of work in a large pit filled with loose blown sand. Prof. Petrie noticed the site when he was excavating the Royal Tombs, and decided to clear it as soon as possible. The opportunity presented itself in the season of 1901-2, and the writer was placed in charge of the work.

On December 14th, 1901, with some fifty men, excavations were commenced at the four points where artificial mounds indicated the existence of ruins, that is to say at S 9, S 10, and the two halves of S 8. Shortly after this the presence of a brick wall just below the sand was noticed to the westward, and this being followed out, the great *hôsh*, or courtyard, was discovered and the clearance of this, and of the great tomb within it, occupied the better part of the season's work. The number of workmen was doubled, and a very large force of boys from the neighbouring villages was engaged for the purpose of carrying the sand and rubbish. As the work advanced in the large tombs these boys were formed up in long chains from the digging level to the surface, each one being a foot or so higher than the last. The baskets when filled with sand were handed from one boy to another until they reached the top, where several were waiting to run with the loads to a suitable distance. The empty baskets were then thrown to the bottom of the pit, and refilled by the trained diggers. These latter, who were paid in proportion to the cubic measurement of their day's digging, speedily overcame the difficulties presented by the falling sand, and worked with a most invigorating "swing," which seldom failed to arouse the energy of the local boys as well.

22. The great *hôsh* is rectangular in form,

and lies along the foot of the cliffs, where the sand slopes down with a clean surface, here and there broken by a large boulder. The wall is constructed of unbaked bricks, usually measuring about 12″ × 5″ × 4″—this being the measurement of the bricks used all over the site. It is about 8 or 9 feet broad, and on the three upper sides of the rectangle it stands from two to four feet high. The lower side, which may be termed the front wall, stands somewhat higher; but it is probable that even the highest walls have lost several feet by natural decay, although there is a complete absence of brick rubbish around them. The hôsh is entered by a fine causeway between two brick piers jutting out from the front wall; this points exactly to the centre of the enclosure. As will be seen on the plan, this causeway begins with a stairway, on one side of which—and perhaps originally on the other also—a number of chambers stood (S 6). The walls of these are only a foot or so in height, but the mass of brick rubbish shows that they were full-sized rooms, as it is natural to expect. The inner face is generally whitewashed; and from the amount of broken pottery found, it appears that the chambers were used as a store place for offerings. No household utensils were found to confirm the otherwise likely supposition that they were the dwelling-places of the workmen or guards employed at the cemetery. The stairway consists of an inclined platform with broad shallow steps built in the middle line, each step being not more than three inches high. It must have been covered up very shortly after the funeral, as the surface, which is whitewashed, is in a very good state of preservation.

Passing up this stairway the entrance is blocked a few yards further by a "wavy" wall, of that peculiar form found on this site. Only one layer of brick remains, and it cannot ever have been high. Further on, as one approaches the hôsh, a platform is found leading up to the entrance. It is askew to the rest of the walls,

and points to the southern half of the enclosure, that is to say, away from the mouth of the great tomb, which is in the northern side; it has evidently been so arranged in order to set plunderers on a wrong track. On either side of this are the remains of a brick construction, apparently also a kind of platform or flooring; and by the right hand pier is a little chamber, evidently a watchman's shelter, in a corner of which the burnt bricks indicate that a fire had been often lighted. A few feet from the end of the "skew" platform stands a square box-shaped building of brick, which was probably the basis of an altar, or a basin of water for purposes of purification. To the right and left of this central point "wavy" walls, now about a foot high, run to the corners of the front wall.

The whole length of the great causeway, in which the axial points are the altar and the stairway, has been laid out originally by sighting towards the west, to a promontory of the cliff behind the back or upper wall of the courtyard. This promontory is surmounted by two large boulders, and being a clear land-mark for miles around, it has been made the axial point of the whole cemetery. Towards the east the causeway runs down in line with the centre of a small temple on the edge of the cultivated land, some 760 yards from the stairway. The temple was excavated in 1900 by Mr. Randall MacIver, and in it was found the lower part of a seated statue, in quartzite sandstone, of a king whose cartouche appears twice as (𓏺𓆄𓎡𓎡), Ra-kha-kau, whose date will be discussed later. A roadway can just be discerned leading from the temple to the beginning of the cemetery buildings, and this, coupled with the fact that the centre of the temple, the causeway, and the centre of the hôsh are all in one straight line, shows almost beyond doubt that the temple and the tomb were built at the same time, and in direct connection with one another.

23. Under the cliff promontory, that is to say, behind the back wall of the *hôsh*, excavations were made to discover whether an entrance to a rock tomb lay there, the position of the real tomb being then still unknown. At a depth of a few feet brick rubbish was observed, and when a small brick enclosure was laid bare the hopes of all concerned rose high. This building (S1) consisted of three chambers, the walls of which stood from two to four feet high, the southern chamber having had a mud flooring. Digging under the floor level of the largest of the three divisions, a pier of rock was seen to jut out from the cliff some 30 ft., apparently artificially trimmed, to a rounded surface. Stonecutters' chisels were certainly used here, for a quartzite stone fragment on which some copper instrument had been sharpened was found. Exactly upon the top of this pier five brick pole-supports were found arranged in symmetrical order, one more having, no doubt, completed the original set. They had apparently been used to support wooden pillars or poles, for each had a circular hole in the centre into which a pole could be thrust in order to stand upright. If the room had been roofed, these poles might have been employed to support the rafters; but their position to one side of the chamber and not in the middle is unfavourable to this supposition. Considering the fact that they lie almost exactly in the line of axis of the whole cemetery it seems more likely that they were the flagstaffs placed above the tomb, which ran not very far from this spot, though over a hundred feet of solid rock lay between it and the surface. Such flagstaffs are represented in tomb paintings, &c., and are thought to have been the masts of the funeral vessels which brought the bodies across the Nile, or at any rate to have been derived from this. The excavations in this quarter were abandoned when it was seen that the entrance to the tomb was elsewhere.

Another brick construction which ought, perhaps, to be recorded, lay to the south of this enclosure. Here, from behind the back wall of the *hôsh*, plunderers had built an unmortared wall forming a rectangle, and within the court-yard a small straight wall running for some twenty feet. Excavations, however, revealed nothing, and it is to be presumed that the plunderers, who invariably built walls to hold the sand back from the mouth of a tomb-shaft, were mistaken. It is, too, about this spot that the "skew" platform points, and it may be this that misdirected their work, exactly as the original architect had intended.

24. To the right of the causeway, and close to the store chambers there was a large pit, later known as S 9, with sand rubbish thrown high up around it. This was the spot where M. Amélineau began to excavate, and here the earliest work of the season was centred. When completely cleared the tomb was found to be of extremely interesting design, and although all portable antiquities had been carried away by the plunderers who had ransacked the place, the architectural features more than justified the labour expended upon it. The plunderers had torn away all the roofing of the passages, and the whole of the inner workings of the tomb were therefore exposed when the sand had been removed. The construction was as follows:— A large pit was first dug through the hard sand, and at the bottom of this the passages were laid out, being built of smooth limestone blocks, usually about 4 ft. by 3 ft. by 2½ ft. The entrance was roofed by a single limestone block [now overthrown] 8 ft. by 3½ ft., arched on the under side, and standing originally, no doubt, on two side blocks. This was some 10 ft. from the surface. Passing it a sloping passage was entered, 3½ ft. wide and probably about 4 ft. high, which ran down until the way was blocked by a huge quartzite sandstone portcullis, which had been let down from above by the knocking away of the supports, as soon as the mummy had been placed at rest. Behind this the passage continued for another four feet, and then opened out into a square chamber, 7 ft. by 10 ft., and of a comfortable height. The walls were solid all round, and to a person attempting to enter the tomb, had he managed to pass the portcullis, the way would now be barred.

Half the floor, however, of this chamber was false, and by removing the slab, which slid in 5 in. grooves, a passage running to the north at right angles was entered. This continued for about 35 ft. and then turned to the west, and a few feet later to the north again, where it seems to have been blocked by a limestone portcullis. After another ten feet or so the passage turned again to the west, and finally to the south. Here a portcullis made of a thin upright slab of quartzite sandstone had to be passed. Behind this the passage became narrower but somewhat higher, the floor being at a lower level; and after seven feet it ran up against the lid of the sarcophagus, which, like the portcullis, had been let down from above.

The sarcophagus was constructed in three blocks of quartzite sandstone. The lower part was one large block hollowed out to a rectangle sufficiently large to hold the coffin, and beautifully trimmed inside, the outer surface being rough-hewn. At the south end, i.e. behind the head, a box-like recess was cut for the purpose of holding the objects buried with the mummy. Two-thirds of the sarcophagus was covered by one block, arched inside and fitting neatly upon the lower part. This was fixed in place when the tomb was built, and was heavily cased around with limestone blocks, through which, had it been possible to break, the sarcophagus might have been reached from the false-floored chamber. For it will be observed that the passage had made a complete turn, and had led one back again towards the entrance. The lid over the open end of the sarcophagus, as has been said, was dropped into place after the body had been placed inside. A small passage not more than 20 in. wide and 2 ft. high branched off from under the passage which ran below the

false floor, and led to the side of the lid; and it was, no doubt, from here that a man broke away the supports and thus closed in the body. The work, however, was not well done, and the lid remained gaping at one end. The plunderers entered by smashing a hole with crowbars between the two lids, and the falling stones must have reduced the coffin to matchwood. Certainly the *débris* shows that the pieces were used as fuel for fires.

It appears that when the tomb had been laid out and the passages and sarcophagus securely covered in with a casing of limestone, the pit was carefully packed with sand and gravel up to the surface level of the desert. The sand was held back from the actual entrance by a brick wall, about eight feet high, whitewashed on the inner side; and a brick staircase led down the box-like shaft at one corner. After the funeral this, too, was filled in, and all trace of the building was obliterated. Upon the surface a square enclosing-wall of brick was then built, and on the east side, or front, a small "wavy" wall formed a frontage. The sand packing was finally raised, perhaps a few feet above the desert level, being held in by the brick wall, and possibly roofed over with bricks, though that is not likely considering the size of the area. The tomb was therefore a mastaba, or at any rate its design was an extension of that idea; and when complete it must have appeared as a low square of brickwork, with possibly a courtyard in front.

25. To the north-west of this mastaba and not far from the north-east corner of the great *hôsh*, another pit surrounded by sand heaps indicated the presence of a plundered tomb. This was known as S 10, and proved to be somewhat similar in form to that just described, and to have been built upon the same principle. Upon the east side a brick shaft, descending by six steep brick steps, led down to the entrance. A limestone passage, 3½ ft. wide, sloped straight down from here, a distance of 20ft., opening out

into a chamber so smashed that it is hard to say what was its original shape or size. It appears, however, to have had a false floor, through which one descended on to a staircase leading to the north. This staircase is peculiar: there is a sloping limestone passage about 3½ ft. wide, and down the centre of the flooring shallow steps have been cut, not more than 20 inches wide, thus leaving a margin of 11 inches or so on either side. The roof does not seem to have been very high, but the passage has been so battered by the plunderers in their successful attempt to rob the tomb, that it is difficult to tell. It runs about 26 ft., and then turns sharply off to the west. A couple of yards further a great quartzite sandstone portcullis, similar to that in S 10, has been dropped down, and on the other side the passage runs on until it comes to an abrupt end against the quartzite sandstone lid of the sarcophagus, lying somewhat askew.

The lid is a large-sized block, carefully dressed on all sides, but of the sarcophagus not a vestige remains. Extensive digging all around revealed nothing, and it is to be presumed that, as it was securely hidden below the floor level of the passage, it was made of limestone, only the drop-lid being of the harder stone. The plunderers would easily be able to break up the former, and there is, of course, a chaos of limestone fragments lying about from the general destruction of the tomb. The supposition is supported by the fact that the lid is one solid rectangular block, and is not hollowed, as in the case of the sarcophagus of S 20, as though to fit exactly upon a lower piece. Indeed, it is rather a covering-stone, designed to block the passage than an actual lid forming part of a uniform piece of work. Near here some fragments of an inscribed alabaster canopic jar were found, which will be mentioned again later.

As before, a sand packing brought the surface of the tomb to a level with that of the desert, and the brick shaft at the entrance having been also filled, a brick construction was laid out on the top. Along the front of the tomb a heavy wall was built, 3 ft. broad and high, crossing above the entrance passage at right angles. Two buttresses run up against this wall, and form a recess between them, about 20 ft. wide. The sides are whitewashed, and there is a brick flooring, which indicates that this was a place for laying the offerings, as in the case of other mastabas. Behind the 3 ft. wall another runs parallel some 9 ft. away, the inner side of each being whitewashed. At the back of the tomb there is a broad, low wall, but on the north and south sides the cuttings disclosed no brickwork. Upon the desert, 65 ft. from the front wall, a whitewashed brick platform was laid down, 37 ft. long and about 12 ft. wide.

This tomb, then, is also in a manner a mastaba, though the features which constitute it as such are open to discussion. Although there is every reason to suppose that the construction on the surface was in the form of a containing wall packed with sand and gravel, with a court or courts in front, there is actually no evidence which can absolutely prove it. Both this and the previously mentioned tomb show a delicacy and strength of workmanship worthy of the XIIth Dynasty. The limestone blocks are beautifully trimmed, and the manipulation of the hard quartzite sandstone must command one's admiration. It must be remembered that this stone had to be brought from the quarries near Cairo—a distance of 400 miles or more by river, and nine over the rough roads in the cultivation and rougher tracks in the desert. Each block, too, weighs several tons. The design of the tombs, on the other hand, was not brilliantly conceived, although it was so beautifully executed. It seems almost childish that so much care should have been expended upon the blocking of the passages leading from the entrance to the sarcophagus, when that entrance was so nicely hidden that a plunderer would be sure to miss it and to attack the building from the top. This is what actually happened, and by a process of digging and smashing, he very possibly landed first shot —if the expression be permitted—upon the treasure he was seeking.

26. To the north of S 10 and east of S 9, there are three smaller tombs constructed upon a uniform plan. The most westerly of the three runs down from the surface as a sloping passage or chamber of whitewashed brick, 3 ft. wide and 10 ft. long. At the bottom a limestone slab fixed into a brick doorway originally blocked the way. This was the entrance to a second chamber with a barrel-shaped roof of whitewashed brick, which had, of course, fallen in. The chamber was 4 ft. wide and high enough in the centre for a person to stand upright. It was 8 ft. long, and ended against another limestone slab. Behind this was a clean drop of a couple of feet into the burial chamber, which had been originally roofed like the second chamber. It was 10 ft. long, 4½ ft. wide, and about 8 ft. high, the walls white-washed. Four slabs of limestone seem to have encased the coffin, and there may have been a fifth placed across them as a lid. One inlaid eye from the coffin was the only fragment of burial that remained.

The middle tomb contained four chambers. The first sloped down from the desert surface for 7 ft., being about 4¼ ft. wide, and having two small steps at the mouth. The second chamber was the same width, and sloped for 8 ft., at the end of which a doorway, barred with limestone, led into a roofed chamber, 9 ft. long and 4¼ ft. wide. Through this a second doorway opened on the sarcophagus, constructed as before of loose limestone slabs, in which a few male bones were found. All the walls of the chambers were whitewashed. The last of the three tombs had only three chambers. The first was 3½ ft. wide, and ran down for 10 ft.

to the next division, 4 ft. wide and 9 ft. long, and roofed as before. Again a door blocked with a limestone slab led to the burial, in a room 10 ft. by 5½, roofed, and containing the remains of a sarcophagus similar to those described above.

These three tombs, it will be seen, contained two roofed chambers led down to by others unroofed. Bricks were heavily stacked above the barrel roofs, and the whole was covered by sand to the desert level. The unroofed chambers were, after the funeral, filled with sand until the building was hidden from sight. The tombs were much destroyed by plunderers, and the roofs had all fallen in, though sufficient remained at the sides to show what shape they had been.

At the extreme north of the cemetery there is a small isolated tomb, S 16, built probably at a later date than those already mentioned. It is rectangular in form and consists of only one chamber with a barrel-shaped roof, through a hole in which the tomb was originally entered. The chamber is 9 ft. long, 3½ wide, and about 5 ft. high, the floor being about 9 ft. from the desert surface. Along the east side a semi-preserved body of a woman lay upon its back, with the arms to the sides and the head towards the north. The tomb had been disturbed by plunderers, and the skull was found at a higher level, having been removed, no doubt, in the search for necklaces or neck-jewels. In the north-west corner there was some undisturbed pottery, consisting of four long jars, three dishes, a few broken saucers, and a fine red polished vase. Their shapes and their position in the tomb are recorded in the plates.

At the south side of the cemetery there is a group of four tombs, known as S 13, 14. They each consist of a rectangular whitewashed brick shaft, running down 9 ft. or so, filled with sand ; but one has a second chamber with a barrel roof, leading from the shaft by a brick door. Practically nothing now remains of the burials.

In one, however, some loose carnelian beads and a scarab were found; and in another there were a few male bones, and some pieces of cartonnage. To the east of this group is a large tomb, built on the exaggerated plan of S 2. The roof was barrel shaped, and some of it was still standing until excavated, when it fell in. Upon the whitewashed walls of the burial chamber a number of drawings of boats had been scratched in later times, some of which are of interest. Photographs of them are given in the plates. At the time of writing this tomb awaits complete clearance, and a fuller description of it will be appended.

27. One of the most interesting features of the whole cemetery is a large building in the form of a double mastaba, which lies just south of the *hôsh* entrance in the corner formed by the great front wall and the left pier of the causeway. Here stands a large rectangular brick enclosure, 69 ft. from side to side in one direction, and about 56 ft. in the other. On three sides the walls are some 5 ft. broad and on the south the fourth wall is nearly 10 ft. They are still 10 or 12 ft. high in parts, which is probably little short of their original size. Like all mastabas the walls have a strong batter, that is to say, they lean towards the centre and if continued to a finish would form a pyramid. The outer surface is regular and well preserved; but the inner, being merely to retain the filling, is quite rough. Across the south end of the space enclosed there is a brick construction in the form of a wall 6 ft. broad, and a series of layers of brick rising like steps, and forming a casing over the *débris* which lies below.

Parallel with this mastaba, with the same line of frontage, is a second enclosure. Its walls are 4½ ft. broad, and its area is about 64 ft. square. A passage 10 ft. wide separates the two buildings from each other. In front of them runs a great fender wall of the "wavy" type, having a batter, and rising some 12 ft. high. Between this fender wall and the front wall of the mastabas a corridor is formed 4 ft. wide (or 8 ft. measuring from each recess or "wave" in the fender wall) running from the corner of the second enclosure to the outside of the causeway wall. At the north-west side of the building, i.e. in the corner, there are a few chambers with strong brick walls; and in one of these the skeleton of a man was found lying full length.

Excavations were made at the centre of the two enclosures, where it was evident that the plunderers had commenced their attack. The filling of both buildings consisted mainly of limestone chippings, but having dug through this at several points nothing but a clean sand bottom was found, in which a deep hole showed where the plunderers had made their vain attempt to find a burial. Further excavations having produced no better results, the work on the site was suspended, and a thoughtful examination of the place undertaken. The conclusions drawn from it changed the whole course of the work, and led directly to the finding of the great tomb in the *hôsh*. It was observed that the limestone chippings were not entirely mason's waste from the dressing of the limestone blocks in the other mastabas. Much of the stone was of a kind too soft for building purposes, and coming evidently from rock cuttings. Among these chippings there was sufficient *débris* to indicate that the rubbish from the whole cemetery had been thrown here. Pieces of rope, granite pounders, pottery fragments, clay sealings, stones used for sharpening copper tools, parts of old baskets, fragments of cubit measures, quartzite sandstone chippings, a mortar for mixing cement, blocks of wood, and so forth, may be mentioned among the heterogeneous objects brought to light. Moreover the strata of the rubbish showed that much of it had been brought up from the direction of the *hôsh* and tipped over towards the south. From all this and many minor indications it was decided that there must be, as had been expected, a tomb cut through the rock, at no great distance away. Excavations under the cliff promontory, as has been described, were already proving hopeless; and a thorough clearance of the *hôsh* was commenced.

It was thus evident that both these two supposed tombs which had proved so fruitless, were in reality great rubbish heaps enclosed and cased in with brickwork to represent mastabas, the "wavy" fender wall being a further protection against prying eyes. In this way the ancient architects believed that they could hide all trace of the chippings which would so plainly tell of the existence of a great rock tomb. The manner of defence usually employed against the plunderer was that of setting him upon a false scent, with a view to disheartening him by much wasted labour. These two dummy mastabas would be the largest visible buildings in the cemetery, and the plunderers would be sure to attack them first; and no doubt the ransacking of the place kept many a gang of robbers out of further mischief.

28. Amid the rubbish a number of grey clay sealings were found heaped together a few inches below the brick covering. They are chiefly scarab impressions of an ornamental character, and are all of the style prevalent in the XIIth Dynasty. The clay was thumbed into the necessary shape, and from the impressions on the under side one is able to see that it was used to secure bands of string or cord at the point where it was knotted. In some cases minute fragments of the string still remain, and the original seems to have consisted of papyrus twisted cord about $\frac{1}{8}$ in. thick, thin strands of linen twine, twisted cord about $\frac{1}{8}$ in. neatly twisted, linen cord about $\frac{1}{16}$ in., and plain untwisted cord about $\frac{1}{12}$ in. There is also upon many of the sealings the rounded impression of papyrus, and on one some shreds of that material are to be seen. From this it seems that the sealings were used to fasten the rolls of papyrus

containing, perhaps, instructions from the royal officials to the overseers in charge of the work at the tomb shaft and elsewhere. It is evident that the seals were broken and thrown aside in the cemetery, and were finally carried across to the rubbish mound along with other *débris*.

There are four sealings which give the names of these royal officials. The first is inscribed *mer seten àpt Ȧy*, "Superintendent of the King's estate, Ȧy"; the second *àri ne Khenu Senb*, "Guardian of the court, Senb"; the third *Nefer-Ka*, without a title; and the fourth *mer net zat mer ḥet urt* VI *Imeru*, "Mayor of the City and Vizir, Superintendent of the six great temples, Imeru."[1] Now the Vizir Imeru-Nefer-Ka is known from a statue in the Louvre, and he lived during the reign of Sebek-hetep III, of the XIIIth Dynasty. Senb and Ȧy are, therefore, probably of this date; and many of the scarabs appear to belong to the XIIIth Dynasty. If, then, there was not another vizier of this name, it is evident from this that the roofing of the "dummy mastaba" was undertaken in the reign of Sebek-hetep III. The small tomb, S 16, may also date from this reign, as we have already seen that the pottery found in it was later than the XIIth Dynasty. The "wavy" walls throughout the cemetery may also have been built by Sebek-hetep, and this is further indicated by the fact that one of them is built right across the entrance to the *hôsh*, [see paragraph 2] which is not likely to have been done at the time of the funeral. We cannot, however, attribute more of the work in the cemetery to this date, as there is evidence to show that it belongs to the XIIth Dynasty. King Ra-Kha-Kau, for whom the small temple

---

[1] This sealing has unfortunately been mislaid, and it does not, therefore, appear in the plate.

upon the edge of the cultivation was built, is to be identified with Senusert [or Usertesen] III, whose throne name was ⟨☉🝙⟩; and we must therefore regard this cemetery as having been built by him also. It has been already mentioned that in tomb S 10, a fragment of an alabaster canopic jar was found. The inscription upon this is peculiar in that the legs of the hieroglyphical birds are cut off. The custom of thus mutilating the characters obtained throughout the reigns of Senusert III and his successor Amenemhat III, and is to be noticed upon the objects found in the tomb of the former at Dahshur [DE MORGAN, *Dahchour*, 1894.] It is not unprecedented that a king should have two tombs, and there is nothing unreasonable in the conclusion which the present evidence compels us to arrive at, namely, that this rock tomb at Abydos is the burial place of Senusert III. A fuller discussion, however, will be undertaken when the complete clearance of the tomb has brought to light all the available material upon which to base the argument.

29. The clearance of the great *hôsh* was a straightforward piece of work, as the depth of the digging was regulated by the hard virgin sand which lay from 1 to 3 ft. below the surface, and into which it was unnecessary to cut. A row of diggers was ranged along the south end and worked forward for a few yards, and the cleared area having been examined, they advanced, throwing their rubbish behind them. At this end of the enclosure six small oval pits were found, all of which had originally contained foundation deposits. They were arranged in no particular order, but it is noteworthy that none was found at the north end, near the great tomb. Two were quite empty, two contained a few fragments of rough pottery, one was filled with an orderless collection of beautifully made vases of red polished ware, the shapes of which are noted in the plates,

and the last—that nearest the tomb—contained a bull's skull and leg-bone, three ordinary bricks, a common flint, two balls of clay, and a few small pottery dishes. Traces of blood from the sacrifice were noticed in the congealed sand.

When half of the *hôsh* had been cleared, a second row of diggers was set to advance from the north end; and as the gangs began to approach one another, that is to say, in the middle of the northern half of the enclosure, the virgin sand was lost sight of, and the cuttings began to assume the form of a series of deep pits. Soon the Arabs found themselves all working in one enormous pit, and the system of labour had to be altered. The most trusted of the trained diggers were set to work over the area at the bottom, and two long chains of local boys were stationed on either side to hand up the baskets of sand, which at the top was heaped upon the "dead" ground around. At a depth of some 40 ft. the limestone rock became visible, and at the extreme east and west end of the pit the mouths of two shafts were cleared, running straight down. Parallel walls of brick connected the two, and the work now appeared as a long narrow enclosure, 85 ft. long and about 15 ft. wide, running from east to west, built upon the face of the rock, with the tomb-mouths at each end. Again the diggers were rearranged, and eight or ten men were set to clear the sand from the shafts, each gang having a chain of boys to hand up the baskets.

When this work was completed, the plan of the tomb was found to be as follows:—The eastern shaft, 11 ft. by 14 ft., led down for about 15 ft., and had a rough chamber cut out upon the east side, some 9 ft. to 7 ft. high, with a 4 ft. ledge running round it. Opposite this chamber and somewhat below it a large tunnel sloped steeply towards the west. The roof was slightly arched, and the floor and walls were fairly dressed. A groove, 2 in. deep and

3 in. high, was cut the whole length of the passage on either side, about 3 ft. from the ground. This, doubtless, was connected with the lowering of the sarcophagi into the tomb. The tunnel ran down until it was met by the perpendicular western shaft, at a depth of about 50 ft., that is to say, some 90 ft. from the desert surface. This second shaft was very narrow near the top, but widened out as it opened into the sloping tunnel. Foot holes were cut down its entire length, and it seems to have been used by the workmen; but its necessity, when viewed in respect to its disadvantage as a further help to the plunderers, is not obvious.

The passage now drops sharply, about 4 ft., and passes into a second tunnel, running level towards the west. It was on March 7th, 1902, that the sand was removed from this point, and the way into the tomb opened. A quick examination of the passages and chambers beyond showed that they were more extensive than those in any tomb known in Egypt. The work of clearing away the debris left by the plunderers, of examining the granite sarcophagus which had been seen in one of the chambers, of searching for other hidden burials, and of measuring and planning the place, was thought to be too great an undertaking for that season, which was already drawing to a close. The work was therefore discontinued, the shaft filled with sand to the top, thus completely preventing any entrance, and guards were ordered to visit the mouth at regular intervals to see that it was not tampered with by the Arabs from the neighbouring villages, whose imaginations had been inflamed to the point of lawlessness by the possibility of a find of jewellery.

30. About a quarter of a mile to the south of the cemetery, excavations were made upon a sandy hollow which appeared to be another great tomb. A large pit, as big as that of the great tomb in the hôsh, was emptied, but when brick construction was reached near the bottom, it was decided to leave the work until the next season, as it was evident that another great rock building was about to be disclosed which would perhaps require several months to clear.

In the cemetery there are two Ptolemaic tombs. One, which is completely wrecked, lies near S 2, and may have been an earlier tomb re-used. The other is built inside the hôsh at the south end, not far from the front wall. Three steps lead down to a large rectangular chamber about 15 ft. by 12 ft. The floor and walls are plastered, but not whitewashed, and the roof appears to have been domed, and to have risen above the desert surface, a mound having been formed over it. Not a trace of the burial remains.

It is unlikely that there are more tombs of any kind in the immediate neighbourhood. Thanks to a great rainstorm all the walls within a couple of feet of the surface were able to be located; for the sand naturally dried more quickly where brick wall or other hard matter lay beneath; and for the few hours while the rest of the desert was wet the positions of all buildings below the surface were marked out. Several climbs along the side of the cliffs in search of rock tombs were fruitless, though a few rough drawings in red paint were noticed, dating probably from Roman times. Much broken pottery of this date was observed on the cliffs, and it seems that the plunderers lived, during their work, under the shelter of a terrace of overhanging rocks above the south end of the hôsh.

These Romans were, however, by no means the first persons to be attracted to the site by the prospect of treasure. Mr. MacIver points out in his El Amrah and Abydos, in which he describes the excavations at the small temple of Senusert III upon the edge of the cultivation, that even before the end of the XIIth Dynasty the temple area had been intruded upon by burials, and the XVIIIth Dynasty found it quite wrecked; and we have already seen that

Sebek-hetep III piously patched up the cemetery and hid the *débris*. It would seem, then, that the tomb and its temple did not remain intact for more than a few years, and it is probable that at the fall of the XIIth Dynasty the first raid upon it was organized. From that time to the present day the cemetery has been dug out again and again, no doubt; but the Romans seem to have thrown as much vigour into their work as any of their predecessors. They have left, as we have just seen, a great quantity of pottery behind them, and we found their lamps and vessels inside the tombs.

They seem to have been an organized gang, and to have been led by intelligent men. Laying aside one's natural prejudice against them in view of the damage they have done, one is forced to admire them for the clever and determined manner in which they broke down all obstacles set in their way by the builders of the cemetery. Their work was appallingly thorough, for they have hardly left behind them a vestige of a burial throughout the whole site. We cannot, however, blame a treasure-seeking people, in whose day reverence for the antique was almost unknown, for having attacked a cemetery the richness of which was apparent. As reasonable would it be to blame the architect for his utter failure to secure from damage so important a burying ground.[1]

---

[1] A word of explanation is necessary with regard to the general plan of the excavated area on Pl. i. At the end of the season 1901-2, the writer passed on to other Egyptological work, and did not, as he had originally intended, return to Abydos to complete the clearance of the great tomb of Senusert III. The general survey of the cemetery which was to have been made during the second season's work was, therefore, never undertaken; and the hasty plan on pl. i. does not pretend to be very accurate. Mr. Currelly who took over the excavations, was unable to find the time necessary for so large a survey, as his discoveries in the neighbourhood required his whole attention. But it is hoped that the plan which appears here is sufficiently correct for all practical purposes.

A. E. P. W.

CHAPTER IV.

THE TOMB OF SENUSERT III.

By C. T. Currelly.

31. While most of the men were away at the Bayram *fantasia*, the few who remained were employed in building a row of huts for themselves, and a small one for me, just above the entrance to the tomb of Senusert III. On the last day of the holiday we moved up, in order to be ready to begin work as soon as the others returned from Quft.

During the nine months that had elapsed since the work described in the previous chapter, the great shafts and part of the pit had become completely blocked with wind-blown sand, and it was necessary to begin afresh the long task of clearing this out. Again a long line of local boys were employed, and here and there a Qufti placed with them to improve the general quality. A number of the best diggers filled the baskets, which were then picked up by the digger's boy, tossed to the first of the line, from him to the next, and so on to the end, where smaller boys received them and carried the sand to the edge of the dumping pile, a few yards distant. With good work nine baskets a minute were passed up the steep sides of the slope. A regularity of momentum was maintained by swinging the baskets in time to the singing that went on almost all the time. Woe to the boy who from slowness or absence of mind was not ready for his basket; on it came, ready or not, and usually, after getting a blow on the chest, he had half of the contents come flying in his face. I have seen the most ardent singer reduced to complete silence, by

having a well-directed handful of sand thrown into his open mouth.

To catch a heavy basket of sand and toss it on is not quite as easy as it looks. Towards evening the basket is apt to become very heavy. Those, however, who were clever enough to get the knack of sending it on by merely giving an upward push to the basket, saved the labour of stopping the momentum and starting it anew. In this way the smallest boys we had, two thin little fellows from the desert tribe of Abadis, would be fresh enough to play all evening, while the more stupid local of twice their size would be completely tired out. A photograph of one of these Abadi boys, Saad abu Suleiman, Saad the son of Solomon, is given on plate xlv.

The perpendicular shaft B was cleared first, and as we descended the difficulty increased, so that it proved no easy task. Near the top, ledges had been left, and the men, standing on these, tossed the baskets up from one to another, but lower down there were no ledges. Not only was the wall square at the corner, but the shaft even widened a little as it descended. Yet, in spite of this, these supple fellows would get their heels on slight projections left by the roughness of the cutting, and then by swaying back on their hips into the corner, keep a foothold, and bending down, take the basket from the man immediately below and pass it up within reach of the man over-head. In this way a descent of about fifty feet was made. It would be interesting to imagine a number of British workmen jamming themselves like this, one above another, in the angle of a 50 ft. wall, and quickly lifting tons of sand to the top. The men did it easily without the slightest mishap, and when I made a short strong ladder for use in the other shaft A, the first man who tried it moved with extreme caution.

In the loose sand near the top we found the draught-board figured on plate xl, 17. This is of unusual type, spaces three by seven; on it are some marks, probably connected with the game. This looks as if it had been roughly made by one of the stone-cutters, to be used by the men at work on the tomb.

When we had worked down to where the perpendicular shaft is joined by the sloping passage A, the men were shifted to the other entrance; and, as soon as this had been cleared out, the sand from the bottom of the shaft was brought up the sloping passage, and so to the surface.

At the top of the entrance to the sloping passage, a number of cuttings made on each side showed where the great stone beams had rested, which held up the roof over this passage, and a little below there was a cutting in the side that enabled the workmen to go up and down. These are both shown on the plan, and a photograph is given of an Arab stooping in the stair cutting. As will be seen, the upper end of the passage is considerably under-cut. This was doubtless in order that the great stones used in the tomb should slide down more easily.

Almost as soon as the shafts were reached last year, it was seen that the tomb had been plundered, and that in order to save emptying out the whole pit made in the sand before the rock was reached, the plunderers had kept back the sand by building a loose wall round the mouth of the shaft. This wall we strengthened, and cleared away a quantity of the sand immediately pressing against it, in order to make it safe for the men at the bottom.

32. When we got below what had been cleared last year, a few potsherds began to appear in what was now ancient rubbish. One or two burnt bricks were also found. After two weeks' steady work an entrance was effected, as last year, when Professor Petrie went through the whole tomb, and Mrs. Petrie, Freiherr von Bissing and Mr. Quibell visited most of it. Taking a couple of men with candles I crawled through to the far end of the tomb. This was no easy task; the heat was very great, the air very bad, and only very seldom was it possible to do anything but crawl. We remained in the tomb for a considerable time, as I was anxious to find out as much as possible before anything was disturbed.

The place had been ransacked with the greatest minuteness. Nothing that could be moved had been left, and where moving was impossible, holes had been chiselled. After the great plundering, the place had been left for a very long time, and then others had discovered it and searched through very carefully, but had disturbed things very little. Everywhere smoke marks on the ceiling showed where they had pushed their little flat Roman lamps in as far as possible, in the endeavour to look behind the enormous heaps of rubbish piled up by the former plunderers. It was impossible to ascertain how much the first plunderers had done, but they had evidently dug into the native rock considerably, as the rubbish filled some rooms completely, and about half filled the remainder. Even in the sloping passage a small tunnel had been run back into the rock, just where this sloping passage joins the shaft, in order to be sure that no hidden rooms or passages might be missed.

33. As the inside has been seriously altered, I think the best idea of the form and history of the tomb will be given by attempting to describe the first plundering. Perhaps it might be well

here to say something of the plunderers, for at the very entrance we came on some pottery that had been broken during the long years they had spent in the determined effort to destroy the body of Senusert III.

Almost all that is known of this pottery was discovered by Professor Petrie when excavating at Abadiyeh (see *Diospolis Parva*). There a number of flat pan-shaped graves were found, and in them a quantity of pottery very like the prehistoric forms, but showing much rougher workmanship. Most of the beads found in the graves also differed from the known types, and great numbers of flat, oblong pieces of mother-of-pearl were strung together. With these there were also many worn articles well known in the XIIth Dynasty, so it would seem as if these people, to whom Professor Petrie gave the name of Pan-grave people, must have come in at the close of that period. It looks as if a strong barbaric race had arrived as conquerors, bringing with them their household goods and ornaments. If not driven out later, the younger generation probably adopted the ways of the more civilized folk, and so no more of the old things are found.

It is the pottery made by these people that the first plunderers left in the tomb (see pl. xl). Doubtless during the remainder of the XIIth Dynasty the temple connected with the tomb, —described by Messrs. Randall MacIver and Mace in *El Amrah and Abydos*,—was in use, and the site of the tomb known and venerated. Consequently at the fall of the dynasty, so great a tomb would be well known to the conquerors, and certainly one of the first places they would attempt to destroy.

34. When the plunderers got into the tomb they found themselves in a room of great beauty, C. Although it looks long and narrow on the plan, the proportions are extremely good, and the great blocks that formed the sides and ceiling are of the finest white limestone. The long blocks of stone which form

the ceiling are carved to look as if the roof were made of long poles side by side.

The photograph on pl. xliii, shows the pole-roof chamber, taken by flashlight. Unfortunately the film was slightly curved in its holder. The effect of the room is remarkable: long, narrow, and severe, yet the feeling of the cross lines of the cutting, and the proportion of them to the size of the room, is such that the few who saw it were strangely impressed by its beauty.

Near the end of this pole-roof chamber, two passages run off to right and left. Each leads to a room, D,D. These rooms are not lined, but the rock was very carefully dressed and then roughly polished. As the two rooms are alike I shall speak only of the south one in detail. The height at the different corners varies from 8 ft. $7\frac{1}{4}$ in. to 8 ft. $9\frac{1}{4}$ in. It is 8 ft. 7 in. wide and 17 ft. $3\frac{1}{2}$ in. long. The variation in the measurements is very slight, though they are nowhere exact, *e.g.*, the east wall at the top measures 8 ft. 7 in., while at the bottom it is 8 ft. $7\frac{3}{4}$ in.; again the north wall at the top measures 17 ft. $3\frac{1}{4}$ in., and at the bottom half an inch more.

With these three rooms the tomb apparently ends. It was quite evident that there were no openings from the side chambers, so these were left. In the pole-roof chamber, however, at intervals of every few feet holes had been chiselled through the thick lining. Usually the place selected was where two stones joined, and with very narrow chisels the corners were cut off, and the stone worked through. Both sides and the end showed nothing but solid rock behind the lining. Next the ceiling was tried. When the great carved blocks at the end opposite the entrance had been broken through, masonry was found above, and when that in turn was torn away, still more masonry, and so on through several layers, till at last the plunderers found themselves in an enormous passage running parallel to the pole-roof chamber, but on a higher level.

35. This passage is lined on both sides with large blocks of quartzite sandstone or granite. One block measured 7 ft. 7 in. × 4 ft. × 3 ft. 6 in. Many of the blocks had been re-used from other buildings and were put in without any idea of regularity, but with a view to hindering any who might wish to get behind them. These once in place and well mortared were practically immovable. Behind the first row masonry could be seen, and an immense amount of labour had been spent on trying to move out a block, but though each one showed signs of having been attempted, there had been no success.

On the left-hand side of the passage the blocks were much smaller, and a few small ones had been shifted enough to prove that no opening ran into the rock on that side.

36. The great attempt had been made at the end, and here the plunderers were successful. The blocks were removed, and behind them a wall of fine white limestone was disclosed. When this was broken through, the plunderers found themselves standing high up near a ceiling, and looking down into a deep well-like room, 18 ft. 7½ in. high.

The room was lined with the same white limestone as was used in the pole-roof chamber. The stones of this lining were fairly large; 5 ft. 11 in. long by 3 ft. 5 in. high, and 1 ft. 7¾ in. thick were the measurements of one of average size. The blocks had been mortared into position, and then the final dressing done so that the chisel passing over the stone and the very thin layer of mortar at one blow gave the effect of fine continuous stone, and hardly showed the joints.

From this an open passage, G, led into a room, H, which was the exact duplicate of room F. The passage connecting these two was cut and roughly polished, like the chambers on either side of the pole-roof chamber.

Here was an end of things for the third time. Again the narrow chisels had been systematically put to work at the corners of the blocks. Every few feet on the walls of room F a hole was cut, only to find the grey native rock behind. Then the next room, H, was worked over in like manner. At last behind a block right up at the roof, granite was seen behind the facing.

37. When this had been found the whole of the lining was stripped from that part of the room, and the granite was seen to be a huge plug blocking the mouth of a passage. The chisel and stone pick had now work on a large scale, for it was decided to cut away the rock from under the great block of granite, and so drop it into the room beneath. At last the great stone, which must weigh nearly forty tons, was undermined and came crashing down into the room. A flashlight photograph of this stone is shown on pl. xliii. The passage was not open yet, for another plug was seen behind where this one had been. As the plunderers found it impossible to undermine this stone and so bring it down, a tunnel was run under it. The stone had its long axis down the slope I, and proved to be a block of about thirty-six tons. Still the passage was by no means open, for behind this there was more granite, and again, as the tunnel proceeded, more and more, till at last the final block was passed 64 feet from the outer end of the second block. After the second, the blocks were a little shorter and were in pairs, one over the other, no doubt from the utter impossibility of moving a block of full size, down a passage not more than three or four inches larger than itself. As it is I cannot tell how the half blocks were ever put in place, for not more than three men could work at once, except to hold back with ropes, and these three would all have to stand at the upper side.

As far as I could ascertain this tunnel yielded the plunderers nothing; when they had passed the last plug nothing was found but the solid rock; and it must have taken a considerable time to make even the small burrow, that enabled a man lying on his side to push slowly forward.

38. Evidently the passage led to some room, and as they had failed by tunnelling under the stone plugs, they next tried making a great tunnel parallel to the passage and a little to the right of it. This was made very large, with the evident intention of making certain of hitting any branch that might run off from the plugged passage.

As the tunnel proceeded the plunderers cut holes through at intervals, to see if they were keeping in line with the granite blocks. When they found that they were getting the tunnel somewhat of the same length as the plugged passage, it was widened out and deepened considerably, and in this way they dropped right in through the ceiling of room L.

39. Here they found a small room lined with blocks of quartzite sandstone. These blocks are exactly the height of the room and very thick. This must have made it very difficult to set them in place, as the slightest tilting would cause them to jam. Once in place, however, it was much harder to get them out. This room opened into the long passage marked M. Here there is no lining, and the rock is not finished off with anything like the care taken in the other unlined parts of the tomb, as no implement finer than the stone pick was used.

The room of irregular shape, N, was lined. It opens into the passage that leads to the final room marked O. This last room was very carefully lined with great blocks of the same quartzite sandstone.

40. Which room was pulled to pieces first I could not determine. Perhaps gangs of men worked in all three at once. The room O had all the great blocks that reached from the floor to the ceiling prized out, and here and there holes had been cut into the rock, to see if any carefully concealed openings were behind.

The room N was treated in a similar manner. Of the three rooms the little one marked L certainly must have seemed the most unlikely; in fact, it is little more than a turn from the plugged passage into the one that leads to the final chamber, O. When, however, the lining of sandstone had been removed, the reason why their first tunnel had failed became apparent.

The opening from the room into the plugged passage had been carefully walled up with limestone of nearly the same colour as the native rock, and also the opening was a little above the bottom of the passage, so that a tunnel going to the bottom, even if spreading out there, would just miss it by a few inches. The removal of the remaining lining showed the canopic box let into the wall at the turning into the passage M, and on the other side of the little room the rock had been hollowed out just enough to allow the great granite sarcophagus to be let into it. At last the long years of search were rewarded; they had found the body of Senusert III.

The sarcophagus is made of red granite. The form is good, as will be seen from the plan drawing on pl. xl, and the workmanship extraordinarily accurate; the angles and sides being very exact. The outside only is polished. There was no inscription either on the sarcophagus or on any other stone in the tomb. The enormous lid slid into position in an acute angle groove—in order that it might not be prized up. Consequently, the only way to get at the body inside was to draw out the lid by moving it in its groove. It is one thing to slide a large piece of granite into a space that just fits it, and it is quite another thing to get it out. The method the plunderers used was distinctly skilful. The first thing they did was to cut away enough rock at either end to allow a man to get in to the rock behind the sarcophagus. Next the rock was cut away behind and under the inner side of it, while the weight was held up by some kind of prop. When enough was cut away the props were suddenly knocked out, and the weight of the sarcophagus, suddenly falling back, came on the edge of the lid and so forced it forward and even broke it. Now it was possible for a boy to get in.

The square canopic box was also of granite, but with a quartzite lid. This lid was of the same form as that of the sarcophagus, square at the ends and round in the central part. The grooves for sliding it into place were the same at the sides, but at the end the angle was square.

On this the same method of getting the lid loose was employed, and then the exquisite alabaster dishes were taken out and smashed altogether. The majority of these were of the trussed duck pattern, and were the most beautiful pieces of alabaster I have ever seen. No traces of the body were found, so it must have been taken away.

During this long search the amount of rubbish that accumulated within the tomb was of course very great. This was carried and dumped into the different rooms till most of them were filled. C was half full, both sides of D were tightly packed, as was also the passage leading to each. F, G, and H were completely filled, and E and F so full that it was necessary to crawl in order to get through them.

41. It appears very probable that the great labour expended in trying to destroy the body of the king was due to political changes. If one looks at the importance of preserving the body in order that the *Ka* might have its home, it is easily seen why a new dynasty would be eager to consolidate their power by destroying the bodies of a former line. Senusert, if his body were broken up, would die a second time, and so really cease to exist. Now being annihilated, there was no chance of life, much less of kingship, in the under-world. This rendered it impossible for him to be feared from the under-world, or to be looked upon as a power of any kind, and thus his house would lose one of its chief claims to the throne. No longer was there any chance of people favouring his house in the hope of obtaining his protection in the other life.

The ransacking of the tomb took place probably at the close of the XIIth Dynasty, about 2500 B.C. A year or so would be quite sufficient to fill up the openings once more with wind-blown sand, and the desert would resume its former appearance.

There for twenty-nine centuries this wonderful tomb lay unknown, its beautiful rooms cut and torn and everywhere piled high with wreckage. The long yellow monotonous waves of the Egyptian desert concealed its mouth, and a thousand feet above its inner chambers rose the great cliffs that guard the unchanging flint-paved Sahara, under which Senusert had hoped to lie as quiet and as unchanging.

On these dark brown flints a traveller may see a water-pot broken by one who came there before him, and by its form may know that he came in the days of Roman domination, or when Israel sweated and prayed in bondage, or even a thousand years before Abraham left Ur of the Chaldees. Beneath these were the rooms where the *Ka* was to move secure in its palace-fortress, or to which it might return when satisfied with the offerings and worship of its own temple.

42. In the fourth century A.D. the tomb was again discovered by the Romans. The rubbish in the sarcophagus chamber was dug over and piled up at the sides, and a small hole was dug in the rubbish in the final chamber. For the most part, however, they contented themselves with pushing their lamps in as far as possible and peering in to see what might be behind the great piles of rubbish. The fragment of inscribed pottery shown on pl. xl, no. 15, is from

one of the three or four water-pots broken during their search.

When we entered, as much rubbish as possible was taken from the pole-roof chamber, and then the left hand room, D, was entered. The chain of basket-boys and men passed it up to the surface, and from there it was thrown on the dump heaps. A little of the rubbish from the right hand, D, was also passed out, but as soon as the former was fully measured and planned, we began to pile rubbish in it. F was the next room cleared. The rubbish was put into baskets and carried back to where we were piling it. To move it along the 75 ft. of the passage E, made it necessary to employ the smallest boys who could carry a basket full, for the passage was so piled up that they alone could stand upright.

As soon as one room was cleared it was carefully planned, and then used to hold the rubbish from the room beyond. In the passages, however, the men merely dug and threw up behind them. In this way we worked through the great rooms and passages, which extend nearly 650 ft. into the rock.

43. We followed the first plunderers through every part of their work. They had used every inch of room possible to pile up the rubbish from their tunnels, and all this was worked over as carefully as possible. Even the tunnel they had so fruitlessly dug under the granite plugs had been filled. This was very difficult to clear out, but we had no idea what it was, and so followed it to the bottom. One day while this was being done I came in to find the men in the sarcophagus chamber. They were called back, and sending Ali, the son of Omar, just ahead of me with another candle, I started to work myself down the little tunnel. He wormed himself along in silence till he came to the end of the part that had been cleared, and then nervously pointed up. The rock supporting one side of a pair of the great blocks above us was broken, and it looked as if very little was upholding the great weight. Ali looked at it for a moment and then said, "I have three wives and eight children, and I always have bad luck." Although in my own case these eleven ties to life were wanting, I was not much more anxious to remove any more rubbish from under the blocks, so that part had to be calculated from the other end, when we found the limestone wall that divided the plugged passage from the sarcophagus chamber.

Even while we were working, the sand twice over blocked the entrance to the tomb; so that a long chain of boys was needed to clear the way again; and when the place was left alone to the long steady sweep of the sand-bearing winds, the entrance was soon filled up, and the kindly sand closed from view and preserved one of the largest tombs that is known.

CHAPTER V.

THE TOMB OF AAHMES I.

By C. T. Currelly.

44. In the tomb of Senusert III only a few men could work at once, so as soon as an entrance had been made, the greater number were taken over to the other tomb found last year. This was followed down into the rock and found to be unfinished.

45 One evening, during the time we were clearing out the huge mass of sand from the tomb, I wandered down near the cultivation to examine some remains of Roman farm buildings (see general plan, pl. lxi). The walls of the enclosure were still visible, though worn down to within a few inches of the desert level by the cutting action of wind-blown sand. This sand-cutting must be very rapid, for during a high wind the sand is driven along with such force that I have frequently found it very painful, and have even seen it draw blood. Things were wonderfully in sight, the enclosure walls, the rooms of the house, and the ash heaps could be easily seen. On the ash heaps I picked up a few small objects, a ring, the stem of a delicately made wine-glass, and some pottery.

While examining the walls I noticed a man, with a long gun over his shoulder, coming towards me from the south. The usual evening greetings were exchanged, and after some little talk he told me that he knew a place some distance to the south, where wonderful antiquities were buried, and that if I would go with him he would show me where the tombs were. As every Arab in the country knows where treasure is buried, no notice is ever taken of such reports; but I was anxious to go south along the desert

in the hope of finding traces of early rock-cut tombs high up on the edge of the cliffs.

46. The man came very early next morning, still with the long gun over his shoulder, and as soon as I had called to one of the workers to bring his pick and basket, we started. The spot to which he led was rather less than a mile south of the tomb of Senusert III, and was high up on the cliffs. All the way both cliffs and desert were carefully scanned to see if anything was not as nature left it. When we arrived at the place we sank a pit or two, and found a few potsherds; but this was like the usual Arab story of treasure.

While the pits were being dug I scanned the desert below as carefully as possible, and was soon attracted by some piles of gravel which had been thrown up by the eddy of an ancient torrent.

47. On the way back I went to look at these gravel mounds. They were about 15 ft. high, and were all of natural formation, but just beside one of them a little ridge, not over a foot high, did not seem as if thrown up with the rest by a stream.

A few strokes of a pick, at a spot where it was certain the desert had not been disturbed, showed that only three or four inches of polished wind-blown sand lay on top of the water-laid *gebel*. Though there was nothing at all definite, I felt that the sand west of this few inches of ridge had been disturbed.

Here, even two or three feet down, there was wind-blown sand. A pit was now dug at what appeared to be the edge of this disturbed area, and a couple of feet under the surface we came on some bricks.

48. As far as it was possible to draw off men from other parts of the work, they were set digging and removing the sand from the pit. When the sides of this pit were definitely found, it was measured, and proved to be 45 ft. across. The work had been going on for two or three days, when some quite perfect bricks were found, and on each was the cartouche, " Ra-pehti-neb, beloved of Osiris." Here was the tomb of Aahmes I, the founder of the XVIIIth Dynasty, the soldier who freed his land from the oppression of the Hyksos.

For days and days the long chain of basket boys was at work, and with the boys were placed all the men who could be spared from other sites. As this lifting of baskets requires little skill the more stupid were set to do it. The keen interest of the bright little Qufti boys in th work was very amusing. Sometimes the line would get into a hopeless muddle owing to some piece of stupidity or two boys quarrelling, and it would take some time and a few sharp orders to straighten it out. At such times the youngest of these Quftis, a strong youngster who could not have been more than eleven, used to become extremely fierce and indignant. He would dash to the edge of the pit, scream out the orders after me in voluble Arabic, shaking his fist meanwhile at the delinquents, and, the heavy basket full of sand still on his shoulder, dance about in his excitement. As soon as the line could be restored to working order, by rearranging the boys or stopping the fight, as the case required, his shrill voice would start the song, and the line answered to him in chorus.

49. At last we had enough of the pit cleared to see some pillars with a passage behind them. Further clearing showed that the big pit we had emptied was formed by the falling in of the roof of a large undergound hall, that had been supported by pillars (plate xlix, G).

From this hall ran two passages; accompanied by two of the men I crawled into the one leading east, D. For a few yards the passage was blocked with sand that had come from the hole which was made by the falling in of the roof. As soon as this was passed, we found ourselves in a wide passage, and following this we came to where it was completely blocked by sand.

50. This end, C, seemed as though it must lead to the surface. To test whether it did or not, one of the men began to dig with his hands into the sand. More ran in till it was again at the angle of rest; so the other man was sent back along the passage and up to the surface, to see if he could find the spot on the desert immediately above where we were. After a while he came back and said he could see nothing, so, hastily making a sketch on a potsherd to show the different turnings of the passage, B, I went back and up to the surface. While I was looking for any indications of connection with the tomb below, a round piece of the desert, about a foot in diameter, gave out a strange noise and suddenly sank. This was a great surprise to the few Arabs who had followed me, and who did not know that there was a man digging underneath. It took a few moments for the uneasiness to wear off, and then several men were put to work to clear this out. About a day was sufficient, and we had the real entrance to the tomb, B.

51. Now appeared the extraordinary cleverness shown in the concealment of this tomb. Early kings had built huge pyramids and tried to hide their bodies within them. They had used heavy doors, trapdoors in floor and ceiling, huge granite portcullises, even rooms made of a single stone, which had the enormous lid so arranged that, once in place, it seemed as if nothing could move it. Later monarchs had built great courtyards around the mouths of their tombs, and tried to fortify their bodies behind hundreds of tons of granite. All had

failed. Aahmes determined to profit by the past and to hide himself and his tomb. Nearly a mile back in the desert he had selected these piles of gravel as the most suitable place. Between two of them a very small pit had been sunk, with no more care shown in its construction than is given to the ordinary grave of the country. See plate xlix a and b, and photograph on plate l. From this small pit he had tunnelled a small chamber, C. This was run parallel to the river just as is done in the ordinary graves. This chamber C is so low that it is necessary to crawl on hands and knees in order to get to the end. Now when the puzzle was being worked backwards, it was easy to notice that this chamber was a little longer than the average. This was no doubt in order to deceive by imperfect light any possible plunderers who might think it worth while to dig open such a tomb. Although I could not find it, evidently there had been at the end some kind of plug, to give the appearance of solid rock all around the chamber.

52. Had the end plug been removed the intruder would have found himself suddenly in a well-cut corridor, D. From this two rooms, E and F, open to right and left; and, after running straight for a time, the corridor winds round till it reaches the hall G. It would seem as if the workmen missed their direction, and went on for some time before they were put right.

The ceiling of this great hall is supported by eighteen columns, the mystic nine on each side of the axis. Directly opposite the entrance is the opening to the passage, which descends rapidly and then turns to the right into the final chamber, I.

In preparing the tomb, a circular pit was first dug in the sand, A; then the cutting was made in the soft conglomerate, B. The workmanship of this pit and of the chamber C is very rough and careless. Once inside the corridor D, the workmanship is much better, the walls being carefully cut and finished to the corners.

The first room entered, E, was found to measure as follows: the west wall, 7ft. 3in., the east wall, 6ft. 5in., the north one, 7ft. 2in., and the south one, 8ft. 4in. This shows very inaccurate work, and was the first sign I noticed of the great haste they must have been in when digging the tomb. The diagonal measurements, however, differ by only half an inch. The entrance is 6 ft. high and has a six-inch threshold left in the rock. As will be seen, the other room, F, is no less inaccurate, and here the room is not finished to the floor. In all digging underground the start was made at the top, the ceiling cut, and then everything measured in relation to that. Here only 3 ft. 10 in. had been cut away.

Both rooms were searched over inch by inch. In F nothing at all was found, but in E a half-burnt twisted rope of grass was lying in a corner. This must be a lamp-wick, and is the first definite sign of the method of lighting these great underground cuttings.

The corridor runs straight for a while and then turns to the right. After the first fifteen yards the work was not done carefully, and all along shows signs of being more and more hurried. A bed of soft sand was cut into, and then the corridor sinks, in order to follow the direction of the more easily worked stratum.

53. On each side, just a few inches below the ceiling, the men had cut little niches in the walls. These are more frequent on the right side, as would be expected. These little niches are 6 to 8 inches square, and from 4 to 8 inches deep. On the ceiling just outside each was a patch of black smoke staining. The lamps had evidently stood in the niches with the wick pointing outwards. Sometimes through this the sharp little copper picks had passed where the corners were being finished, and in the patch of smoke is a line of clean rock showing the green particles scraped off the pick. These little holes with smoke marks run all along the corridor from the place where the hurried work began,

and are from 20 in. to 10 ft. 3 in. apart. Sixteen of them are on the right wall, with an average distance of 7ft. between them, and nine are on the left wall, with the average of 7ft. 10in. These, as far as I know, are the only examples of such niches yet found, and certainly prove that the Egyptians used a smoky lamp of some kind. Probably a potsherd or small saucer with a little water under the oil served well enough. Had the tomb been finished quietly these holes would doubtless have been worked out and all signs of smoke obliterated.

Near the hall of pillars the work was left still more unfinished, the corners quite round, and the corridor not dug out to its full size.

54. The great hall must have been very imposing before some earthquake or other disturbance caused it to fall in. The nine columns, three by three on either side, are nearly regular and the little irregularities seem to give a feeling of greater size. Most of the pillars are exactly 4 ft. square, but in some cases there is a slight variation. On the north side of the hall, all three pillars of the east line and the second and third of the middle line had crushed down and so the top had fallen in.

55. Directly through the hall from the corridor is the entrance of the passage descending to the final room, I. For a few yards from the hall of pillars the cutting in this passage is carefully done, but after that the work was merely forcing a hole onward as fast as possible, without any attempt to finish the top, bottom, or sides. In the corridor D, near the entrance to the hall of pillars, the sides and top are quite unfinished, and it would seem as if the first men went on at full speed till they reached the spot where they wished to make the large hall. Here, of course, many more men could be employed at once in digging through between the pillars, while the first gang pushed right on to the room at the end. From the place where the passage left the hall a fresh start was made, and the rock cut carefully right into the

sides and corners. Then everything suddenly stopped.

56. The explanation of this must be that the serious illness of the king caused the work to be pushed on as rapidly as possible, and then his death, coming sooner than was expected, made it necessary to use the unfinished tomb.

The whole tomb was most carefully searched; but the only things found were several small pieces of sheet gold that were lying in the great hall, and some larger pieces that were found just at the entrance, and perhaps lost when the body was removed to his Theban tomb.

57. The next question was where could the hundreds of tons of excavated earth be hidden? It is certain that a man who could plan a tomb with such skill was not going to publish its existence by leaving huge piles of rock chippings exposed in the neighbourhood. Pits were sunk on and round all the gravel piles, to see if the rubbish had been hidden by making piles of chippings of the same form as the natural mounds, and covering them over well with gravel. All the gravel piles, however, proved to be of natural formation.

Some distance up on the cliff stone had been quarried, and there were quantities of stone chippings. Those on the surface were certainly not from the tomb, so a pit was dug to see if under these there might be some from the strata cut through by the tomb.

While the man was digging his boy was carrying the baskets of stone a little to one side and throwing them into a heap. Just a few baskets had been thrown out when he brought back a small scrap of bronze. It was a badly broken head of Osiris. By this time I was satisfied there was no rubbish from the tomb here, so now a new problem presented itself. Quarrymen do not usually carry small bronze images to their work. At once more men were called up and told to clear away all rubbish to the ground.

58. A few hours' work enabled us to see a

large brick wall; and on each brick was the cartouche of Aahmes I, evidently made with the same stamp as those found in the Aahmes tomb.

These walls were so very long, and there was such a mass of rubbish heaped above them, that it took some time to find out what the structure was. When at last it was cleared, we saw that it was a large terraced temple, with a frontage of over 400 ft. (see plan liii). As the structure was on ground sloping steeply, the terraces were supported by two long retaining walls. The first one was of brick built in hollow squares. The inside measurement of one square was 3 ft. 9 in. by 4 ft. 7 in., and of another 3 ft. 8 in. by 6 ft. The top, however, was built over, so that it looked like a solid wall.

The brick wall was 370 ft. long. The height of course varied with the nature of the ground; in one place it was 97 in. high on the inside and 108 in. on the outside. The first terrace was made by filling in with sand to a level with the top of the wall. At certain intervals (see plan) brick pilasters were built on the outer face, and at the two ends there was a wall a single brick thick connecting these. This was about 38 in. high.

The second retaining wall was of rough stone set with a sandy mortar; it is about 160 in. high; but, like the front wall, of course varies with the ground underneath. This wall has a batter of about 2 ft. In the plan two sections are shown that will give an indication of the relative positions and heights of the walls and terraces.

59. Of the great stone temple nothing was left but the hundreds of tons of chippings. Every stone had been carried away to build one of the great temples nearer Abydos—either the one built by Sety I or that of Ramessu II; and our knowledge of the father and son does not leave much room for doubt which saved himself the expense of getting out his own stone. The temple of Ramessu is very badly ruined, and is of

the ordinary white limestone of the neighbourhood, so I could not identify the stone; nor did I find any marks to show that the stone now in place had been recut from an earlier building.

The stones had been recut to suit their new position before leaving the terraced temple. At first I thought that this was only the rough dressing to save the extra weight in dragging them across the desert, but later we came on the place where the fine cutting had been done. On the leeward side of this the depth of the lime dust was 30 in. As will be seen from the plan, the pile of chippings in front of the brick retaining wall is the highest, it is about 160 in. in height.

Aahmes chose for the site of his temple one of the most conspicuous places in the neighbourhood. From the earliest times the high roads have been the great dykes that divide the country. Opposite one of these, and about a third of the way up the cliffs, stood the long white temple.

60. The only thing we could definitely call an entrance was found at the south end of the terrace (see plan, pl. liii A). Here was a paved platform with two steps that led up to the gate. This had a wooden threshold let into the bricks, and the gate or door turned on a stone socket. The court B was brick-paved, and seemed to have had a seat in the angle of the front wall. From this court a sloping ascent led to a higher level where the spaces divided by the brick walls were all paved with a pinkish marl. Part of this sloping way was open, as if it had once been paved with slabs of stone now removed. By stepping across this, the irregular enclosure B was entered, and from there a gate led to the first terrace. This gate, which was of the height of the narrow wall running round the large retaining wall, had certainly not been cut down, so it cannot have been the door of a room.

The part on a higher level, F, G, H, I, and J, looked as if it might have contained a number of rooms, but only about a foot of the walls was standing. The round brick-lined hole at M was probably a pit for storing corn. The long division marked H and J was a little higher than the rest and carefully paved with brick and then stuccoed over. At the end of it was a stone daïs, very carefully cut, and about 6 in. high. The front and two sides were bevelled under, so that the top extended an inch over the base. I could not determine what was the use of this, though it may have been the base of a seated statue. In front of this ran the wall N, which extended right up round the end of the cliff. In the marl paving of these divisions a number of rejected carved stones were found. They had been cut as part of the stonework of the building, and then a crack or some other flaw being discovered, they were thrown in to fill up the platform. These fragments showed excellent work both in the lines and in the care expended on the carving.

61. The great foundation deposit was found just outside the wall at K. We took out nearly two thousand pots and stone model vases. The pottery was very rough. The stone model vases were mostly of limestone painted red, black, yellow, and brown; a few, however, were of alabaster. With these was the gold band shown on pl. xlviii.

Another small deposit was in a shallow pit marked L. Rather below it, to the left, was another. This latter had some little flat dishes set in rows, and in some of them were pieces of incense.

At O, flat pots with lids were set in the order shown. A number of model boats had been placed along the wall to the left of the large deposit of pots, and a few more were found just inside the wall N, but all being of wood had been destroyed by the white ants. Above, along the upper wall of H, model paddles and little sticks were found at very short intervals. There was a regularity in the way they were placed, so a drawing was made of the best set (see pl. xlviii).

Apart from these few things nothing was discovered to give any information about the temple. Perhaps it was built by Aahmes for his own worship; but unless we get it from literary sources we must remain in uncertainty as to what was its architecture and for whose worship it was destined.

CHAPTER VI.

THE SHRINE OF TETA-SHERA.

By C T. Currelly, M.A.

62. While the main body of the workmen was engaged on the Aahmes tomb, a few asked to go to the south of the Abydos Pyramid. A rich tomb had been accidentally found there, and our men were naturally eager to see if there might be any more such. The place proved to be the cemetery connected with the pyramid temple that was excavated by Mr. Mace, and published in *El Amrah and Abydos*. All the tombs were of the XVIIIth Dynasty. A good deal of pottery was found and a few Ushabti figures, the only one of special interest being that of Pa-ari, the keeper of the pyramid temple (see pl. l, No. 8). The small seated figure on the same plate was found, not in the burial chamber, but lying on the floor at the bottom of a shaft. The number of the tombs was very small; perhaps fifteen in all could be accounted for, either from our digging or from Arab plundering.

This little cemetery is very near a modern Arab one, and between the two stands a rather large white Sheikh's tomb. This is greatly venerated by the fellahin, who come in considerable numbers to kiss the four uprights of the wooden box-like cenotaph that stands in the middle of the tomb. I noticed that in walking round it they always kept the right side to the cenotaph, and that a small boy was corrected for going the other way.

Great care is always taken not to violate anything that is held in any way sacred, so our men had been told how close to the tomb they were to dig, and no matter how promising a pit happened to be, it might not be pushed any nearer. Of course, the villagers did not know this, and for a few days I noticed considerable nervousness. There evidently was a fear lest we should dig right under the Sheikh's tomb, or even pull it down. Just as we had exhausted the cemetery, a select deputation of the biggest men in the district, armed with clubs, came up to ask us not to go any nearer. The request was granted at once.

63. Between the pyramid and the Aahmes tomb and temple there was a small mound that had the appearance of being a mastaba. Here and there it showed signs of having been pitted by the Arabs, but had still standing a considerable mass of brickwork. A scratch or two with a pick was made at different distances all along the outside, and showed that just under the surface there extended for some distance, especially north and south, about two inches of brick-dust. The centre of the mound was now about 80 in. above the desert, so it seemed as if the mastaba had been built moderately high. The outer walls had a slight batter, and were fairly thick, as will be seen from the plan (pl. li). It was rather surprising to find that the bricks had the same cartouche of Aahmes as those used in the terrace temple, " Neb-Peht-Ra, beloved of Osiris." The bricks were not quite so thick as those from the temple, and the stamp used for imprinting the cartouche was narrower. I measured a large number of the bricks, and

found the variation in size to be 18·5 × 7·8 × 5 inches to 16·7 × 8 × 4·9.

Around the entrance to the chamber of offerings there were hundreds of offering pots. They were all of the one kind, and, as far as could be seen, were in no particular order; sometimes they were scattered and sometimes piled two or three deep. The great stele was lying near the end of this chamber of offerings (see pl. li).

64. This is one of the best steles I have ever seen. It is seven feet high and of the finest workmanship. It shows Queen Teta-shera seated on a throne. Her head-dress is the vulture with the drooping wings, and in her hand she carries the flail. Before her stands her grandson, Aahmes I, with the heavily-laden table of offerings. The carving is the very best work of the XVIIIth Dynasty, and is both sure and clean.

65. The stele is a dedication by Aahmes to his grandmother: "I bethink me of the mother of my mother and the mother of my father, the great queen and Royal mother Teta-shera, justified, whose tomb and sepulchre is now on the ground of Thebes." Very little was previously known of this queen. She is mentioned in a papyrus now in the Cairo Museum, and was supposed by Erman to be a prince, Teta the little (see *A. Z.* xxxviii, 150). The papyrus places her at the end of the XVIIth Dynasty. In the British Museum there is a small seated figure of her, placed by Dr. Budge as a queen of the latter part of the XVIIth Dynasty.

The statement, "the mother of my mother and the mother of my father," goes a little way towards straightening out the tangle of the families just before the XVIIIth Dynasty. Aah-hotep's first husband, the father of Kames and Aahmes, was then her brother and of the royal line. At her husband's death Aah-hotep married the Berber Se-qenen-ra, and, as there was no daughter in the first family, the

daughter by this marriage, Nefert-ari, became the heiress. In this way Aahmes, who was the direct royal descendant, became king only by virtue of being the husband of Nefert-ari, who may have been of royal blood on the mother's side only.

To this great queen and royal mother king Aahmes built this shrine and the neighbouring pyramid; "My majesty desireth to cause to be made for her a pyramid and a chapel in the sacred land." The reason is expressed at the bottom of the stele: "because he loved her more than anything; never did the kings of former times do the like for their mothers."

66. When the whole shrine had been cleared, the structural walls and divisions were found to be nearly symmetrical. The long walls will be seen to be the same on both sides of the chamber of offerings, but the cross walls vary slightly.

The stele evidently stood immediately opposite the entrance. When found it was lying face up, with the top at least two feet lower than the base. It would seem as if it had been dragged out of its position and partly turned round by plunderers hunting for the *Ka* statues, which they had hoped to find behind it in the inner room. This room, however, was filled with brick rubbish, like the other sections of the structure, and the way in which the bricks lay leaves no doubt that this filling was original.

The walls were substantially built, but are not very true. The whole building is also a good many inches out from squareness. All the rubbish put in to make the sections of the structure solid was cleared out by us, but the only thing found was the broken figure of Renutit, the snake-headed goddess identified with Isis, shown on pl. l. A few scraps of pottery showed that the influence of Mediterranean potters, especially those from Cyprus, was being felt. This type of pottery was very plentiful when we came to dig over some houses in the town, built for the workmen employed on the different monuments erected at this time.

67. The pyramid so frequently mentioned and now shown to have been erected as a monument to Queen Teta-shera, stands in a direct line with her shrine. The French excavators sunk pits into it for some time, but could find out nothing. Mr. Mace then tried to get in by tunnelling and propping, and also failed. Under the outer stone casing the pyramid seemed to be a great mass of loose stones. Mr. Mace tried every possible means to reach the centre. A tunnel was started and props put in, but the material was so loose and ran in so fast that it seemed as if the whole pyramid could be taken out of that hole. After working the whole season at great risk the attempt was given up, and the pyramid retained its mystery.

During the time of these different finds the attempt to discover the hundreds of tons of rubbish from the Aahmes tomb was in no way abandoned, and hardly a day passed without some probing being done, in hope of ascertaining its whereabouts. One day it occurred to me, could that pyramid be a "dummy"? A careful re-examination was made of the different strata cut through by the tomb, in order to thoroughly fix each rock well in my mind, and then the pyramid was examined.

Every kind of rock cut through in the tomb was found in the pyramid, and well in proportion to the length of the passage in the different strata.

The piety of Aahmes is now explained. He built the tell-tale rubbish into a stone-faced pyramid, and then built the shrine. In the shrine the grand stele put up for all men to see gives the information that the buildings were for the glory of Teta-shera. Also in order to discourage any hunting for her tomb, which if carried far enough might even lead to the discovery of his own, the stele states that she is buried at Thebes.

The pyramid defied you to say there were not regular chambers somewhere in its centre. You could not tunnel it, nor dig down through it; in fact the only way would have been to remove the whole mass entirely, layer by layer, and as this would have involved an enormous expense, it certainly appeared when Mr. Mace gave up his attempt that we were not likely to have any very definite knowledge about it. Then as the material was from beneath the surface, and so from unknown strata, the chippings could not be identified as coming from any quarter where such rocks were known to exist. Doubtless Aahmes had the satisfaction of feeling that as long as his carefully hidden tomb remained secure, the pyramid would faithfully hold its secret.

68. The town of Aahmes was constructed for the men employed on the different monuments erected in connection with the tomb. It was built on one design, with certain walls running right through the whole length. These walls were very well built; and very thick, as will be seen from the plan, pl. liii. The season came to an end before more than a quarter of it had been dug over.

The town had been inhabited for some time and then abandoned, and after a careful search I could find signs of re-occupation in one room only. Here another floor had been tramped hard about 20 in. above the former one. Signs of re-using the rooms, or of long use of them, were carefully sought for, to determine if the things found in the different rooms could serve as being accurately dated. If no long use was proved, anything found must be fixed to about ten years, 1580—1570 B.C. With this in view every room was carefully examined and the contents worked through; and I feel quite certain that this exact date may be given to everything found in the rooms.

The pottery was mostly of the red polished ware, so characteristic of the dynasty. Many flat dishes were found with the ornament incised, (see pl. lviii, 1, 2, 3, 4, and 5), and there was some of the black incised ware, 6 and 7. A most interesting set of fragments showed strong Cypriote influence (pl. lviii, 8, 9 and 10); but the most interesting find of all was the neck of a false-necked vase, No. 11 of the same plate. This is the kind with the moderately light yellow slip, and the black very deep and glossy in colour. Another fragment of the same vase was found, but though I offered a good reward for the other pieces, we did not get any more of it. This is, I think, the earliest specimen known of the false-necked vase to which a definite date may be given.

Clay toys were moderately plentiful; and, as will be seen, the majority of the dolls have holes by which hair might be attached to them.

On pl. xlviii are shown the designs from the examples of blue-glazed pottery that we found. There were great numbers of fragments of this ware in every room, but they were mostly without ornament.

In the store-rooms we found a considerable number of the store jars still in place. One of them was about two-thirds full of ointment. When found it was caked quite hard, but after being put in the sun for a few hours, it melted.

The plan will be found to explain the two large houses and the store-rooms quite well. The houses are semi-detached and very nearly alike. House 2 has been altered slightly after it was built.

Had we been able to dig over the whole town we should probably have obtained more information and antiquities from the small houses of the workmen; but this was impossible owing to the season coming to an end.

69. Dr. Spiegelberg has very kindly examined the ostrakon, and favoured us with the following account of it:—

"The hieratic text, whose facsimile and hieroglyphic transcription is given on pl. liv, is written in red ink upon white limestone ($0,20^{m}$ × 0,23). The rather rough style of writing may well belong to the XVIIIth Dynasty. The title, 'To inform you about the objects left behind (deposited?) with me in the village,' shows that we have before us a business letter. The whole of the *recto* is occupied by the detailed enumeration of these 'objects.' There are among them, '3 sacks (*medimni*) of barley, 1½ sacks of wheat, 29 bushels (*ḥrš*) of onions (? *ḥḏ*)' Among the other objects, introducing some new words into our dictionary, a good many are obscure. There are objects of wood and of stone, among which I quote, 'a box, two legs of a foot-stool, 12 bricks of natron, 1 door and 2 pieces (? = שתרה) of sawn wood.'

"The *verso* begins thus: 'The things that are with *Pᵉshᵒdᵉ* and *Shᵉryᵉt-Rᵉᶜ* (fem.), they are all written down.' Whether this refers to the enumeration on the *recto* I cannot decide. It continues with this private communication for *Shᵉryᵉt-Rᵉᶜ*, 'Let *Amᵉn-ᶜm-wᵉ* dwell in my house, that he watches it. Write how you are!'

"The last phrases sound as if the writer had suddenly gone away from home and sent some orders to arrange his affairs.

"The second piece, a red potsherd (Ostrakon 0,09 × 0,02) of about the same date, perhaps a little later, is some exercise piece of a pupil. The compound preposition *ḫft ḥr* is so often repeated in the few extant lines that one may guess that the pupil has studied upon this piece the use of that preposition."

CHAPTER VII.

THE INSCRIPTIONS.

By Alan H. Gardiner.

70. The inscriptions published here for the first time are comparatively few in number, but cover the whole range of Egyptian history. The earliest dynasties have yielded a number of sealings, which, while multiplying the problems attaching to this obscure class of texts, at the same time afford fresh material for their solution: among them is the record of a hitherto unknown king Sekhemab Perenmaat. The Vth and VIth Dynasties are not represented. From the Middle Kingdom there is a biographical fragment of considerable philological interest, and a stele containing the names of many relatives of Queen Auhetabu (XIIIth Dynasty). The stele of Aahmes I, which narrates the building of a cenotaph at Abydos for his grandmother, Teta-shera, takes rank as one of the most fascinating official monuments surviving from Pharaonic times. Besides this, a few steles and miscellaneous objects must be attributed to the XVIIIth Dynasty. The remaining dynasties have given nothing of importance: some funerary texts from the tomb of Hordauankh (XXth Dynasty), a few canopic jars, and various short inscriptions. The Ptolemaic and Roman times have left but a few odd fragments.

71. Inscriptions of the earliest Dynasties.

Pl. i, 15. Stele of a woman, inscribed with her name (?). Ist Dynasty.

ix, 2. Fragments of the sealings from the reign of Perabsen, published, *Royal Tombs* ii, 22, 184, 185.

3. Sealing of a hitherto unknown king, Sekhemab Perenmaat. Of the two names, Sekhemab is doubtless the Horus name, Perenmaat the personal name. Both are placed within the square, in pursuance of a custom which obtained throughout the Old Kingdom, and which we find first exemplified in the case of Khasekhemui (cf. Sethe, *Untersuchungen* iii, p. 37). Sekhemab is, curiously enough, the Horus name also of Perabsen, whose personal name, too, closely resembles that of Perenmaat. It is clear that a place must be assigned to the new king at no great distance from Perabsen and Khasekhemui. The words between and outside the squares will be the titles of an official, since the hieroglyphs face in an opposite direction to the royal names. 𓏏𓎢 is unintelligible, but 𓂋𓈖 and 𓁹 are of course the words for "confirm" and "see" respectively. Their sense in the context is, however, far from clear.

8 is a private sealing, and will contain, like other sealings of the kind, epithets and a proper name. 𓊹𓏏 has been discussed by Professor Sethe (in Garstang, *Mahasna*, p. 20), who translates "pleasant teacher." The next signs, 𓂋𓎡𓂝𓏭, must be viewed as a second epithet. 𓂋𓎡 is known from, e.g. *Royal Tombs* ii, 22, 190, where it is probably a participle, "sealing." In combination with 𓂝 𓏭 it may better be interpreted as from 𓂋𓃀𓎡𓅆𓏭, "to make prosperous": cf. Sethe, *Verbum* i, § 178, for

the omission of 𓅮 . The remaining signs, �⌴ 𓅯 , will be the name of the owner of the seal. The whole inscription can thus be hypothetically rendered: "Pleasant teacher, cheering the heart, Karem."

9. Royal sealing of Khasekhemui, with the title of an official, 𓅯 ⬭ 𓎼 𓊪 𓈖, "overseer of the foreign country." This title should be distinguished from 𓅯 ⬭ 𓈖 𓈖, "overseer of the desert." 𓈖 appears always to mean the sandy deserts outlying Egypt, never "foreign country." Where 𓈖 has the latter sense, it should be read 𓎼 𓊪 𓈖, 𓋴 𓊪 𓎼 𓈖: compare MAR. *Mast.* 188, with SPIEGELBERG-PÖRTNER, *Grabsteine* i, p. 1: and for the N. K., NAVILLE, *D. el B.* 79, with *ibid.* 82; *ibid.* 77, with *ibid.* 81. See, too, GRIFFITH, *Hieroglyphs*, p. 31.

10. Private sealing of one Nezemab, the name being twice repeated. The first epithet is partly lost, only the signs 𓇓, "king (?)" and 𓄤, "good," being still preserved. Between the names, four signs, which may be compared with GARSTANG, *Mahasna*, 10, 13. The form of the last hieroglyph here does not favour Professor SETHE's reading, 𓊪𓇋𓄤𓎡.

12. Part of sealing of Aty 𓇋𓂝 (?). See on 13.

13. A private sealing. The fourfold 𓇋𓂝 is presumably the proper name Aty, cf. *Royal Tombs* i, 32, 27, and here 12 (?), and 18. The two birds, twice found between the names, appear to be the eagle sign; but one is tempted to see in them the ⬭ bird, and to render them as the title "the washer." A second epithet is 𓈖 𓅯 𓄤, which we have met previously (cf. above, on 8). To the extreme right occur two names 𓎼 and 𓄤𓂝. Perhaps these were the names of the parents of Aty.

14. Private sealing. Are we to find the name of the owner in the groups Nefermaat, as probably in 24 below, or in the twice recurring 𓏞𓇋𓂝 ? If 𓇋𓂝 in the latter combination is to be understood as "stone," the expression "divine of stone" is strange either as an epithet or as a name. The name of the magician in the Westcar Papyrus, Ubaaner "opener of stone," is an imperfect analogy.

15. Fragment consisting of the word for "East," in its old spelling.

16. The only intelligible words are "life" in its phonetic spelling, and "teacher" 𓈖𓏤𓅯, on which see 8. 13.

Pl. x, 17. Private sealing, twice repeated, belonging to a man 𓇋𓅯𓂝 (?) Two epithets, of which the one may signify "great of monuments," and the other "firm of mouth."

18. Private sealing of 𓇋𓂝 Aty: cf. on 13. Before the name " . . . . . . (⬚), the things of his father"(?) After it the word *nu*, "hunter," which occurs again, determined by 𓈖, in 25. The hieroglyph of the hunter leading a dog may be illustrated, as Mr. AYRTON points out to me, by the very similar sign in the tomb of Methen (L. *D.* ii, 3).

19. Imperfect sealing, the same signs thrice repeated. The name is uncertain. 𓇋𓏠 may mean "his mouth is firm": cf. above 17.

20. Here again the name is uncertain. 𓏠 and 𓇋𓅯𓂝 may be understood as "firm of arm" and "the praised" respectively.

23. Contains 𓈖𓏤𓅯, with which we are now familiar.

24. Private sealing of one Nefermaat—a name which possibly occurs above in 14, and frequently elsewhere. Of the titles, 𓇋𓇋 perhaps means "he of the department": 𓊪𓃒 is known from the great slate palette (QUIBELL, *Hierakonpolis* i. 29): and 𓉐 𓏌 𓃾 is a group found on other early sealings; cf. QUIBELL,

Hierakonpolis ii, 70, 14, 15. Finally, ☥ ⊚ may signify "living, protected."

The present writer wishes it to be understood that the notes supplied above are in nearly all cases entirely conjectural. The time has not yet come for any renderings of these early texts to be regarded as certain; and this being the case, guesswork must at present be suffered to take the place of a more scientific treatment.

72. Pl. xiii. Mr. WEIGALL has already dealt with the stele of Auhetabu, hence it needs no further discussion here.

Pl. xiv. Funereal stele of the Middle Kingdom. The formulae are devoid of interest. The chief persons are Ay·and Useru, and a woman Meres, respectively their mother and wife. Among other persons, two men, Iseneb and Apy, and two women, Atiab and Merkhet, are named.

Pl. xv, 3. Proscynema for an "*uartu*-officer of the table of the prince," a not uncommon title. Middle Kingdom.

6. Proscynema in favour of a [hieroglyphs] ("of the Vizier"). The title occurs elsewhere, but somewhat differently spelt, e.g., [hieroglyphs], *Brit. Mus.*, 208. Middle Kingdom.

Pl. xviii, 3. *Ushabti*-figure of " the overseer of the two granaries, Amenemheb, the son of the scribe Dehuti, born of Nesnub "; inscribed with the 6th chapter of the Book of the Dead. The two vertical lines contain the following words:—" The town god of the overseer of the two granaries, Amenemheb. (It) is placed behind him and in front of him; his *ka* in front of his face every day. It is [hieroglyphs] (an epithet. of Osiris), the true of voice; the overseer of the two granaries, Amenemheb." This obscure formula is known from statues of the Saite period, on which it appears frequently, and with a number of variants; cf. the articles of PIEHL, *Ä. Z.*, 1879, pp. 143 foll.; *ibid.* 1880, pp. 64 foll.; and of NAVILLE, *Ä. Z.*, 1880, pp. 24 foll. The figure here under discussion appears to give the earliest known text. XVIIIth Dynasty.

6. *Ushabti*-figure of the singer of Isis, Pathau.

12. Canopic jar of the same lady. Not earlier than the XXth Dynasty.

73. Pl. xix. At top of plate, four fragments of an obelisk. The fragment on the right gives an epithet ("binding the lands, Horus . . . . . ."), of the Pharaoh who made the dedication: the two larger of the three remaining pieces state that "(he made it as) his monument to his father Horakhti," and "to his father Khepra, lord of the castle," respectively. XIXth (?) Dynasty.

Below, on the left, a block with prayers in favour of " the chief scribe of the king, Tetaty." The wish, " may he (i.e. Horus) grant a good life in the palace in reception of favours every day," is a departure, though one of a not unusual kind, from the stereotyped phrases. XIXth Dynasty.

In the middle, a similar block dedicated to " the scribe of the king Khary," and to " the scribe of the king Amenemheb." The same stone mentions a "singer of Isis, Hathor." XIXth Dynasty.

On the right is an invocation on behalf of " the *aden*-officer[1] of the great corps of Tehen-Aten, Kara." The man is known from a stele published by MARIETTE, *Cat. gén. d'Abydos*, 1062. There is a statue of a " fanbearer of the corps of Nebmaatra (Amenophis III.) Tehen-Aten," by name Kames, in the British Museum (No. 1210).

The words Tehen-Aten, i.e. " the sun-disk glitters," recur in other connections during the reigns of Amenophis III and Akhenaten; a town, a temple, and a dahabeyah, of Tehen-Aten are known besides the corps here so

---

[1] Read [hieroglyph].

named; cf. LEGRAIN, *Ann. du Service* iv, p. 149. The view of M. LEGRAIN, that the temple and town so designated are none other than the temple of Karnak and the town of Thebes (No Amon), has much to commend it; if it is correct, then the corps of Tehen-Aten may well be identical with the corps of Amon, of which we read in the accounts of the battle of Kadesh. End of XVIIIth Dynasty.

Pl. xxii. Canopic jars of the XIXth Dynasty, inscribed with various names and titles: (1) a woman, "the dweller of the town, Astnefret"; (2) a woman, Tabakenast; (3) "the field-labourer Unnefer"; (4) "the *uab*-priest Paunsh"; (5) uncertain; (6) "the workman of Isis, Urshenu." Prof. SPIEGELBERG (*Ä. Z.* xxxvii, p. 37) quotes instances of "workmen" of Amon and Osiris, with which the present example may be compared. Three jars out of the six bear the formula "⌷⸏🯅🯆 the Osiris N.," which is familiar from *ushabti* figures, but very rarely occurs on Canopic jars.

74. Pl. xxiv. 1. Five fragments of an ebony casket, inscribed with portions of at least three speeches made by a king Sety. In 1ᴮ the god Tanen is addressed, in 1ᶜ apparently the gods of Egypt. On the latter fragment the following words are legible: "Sety. He says: Hail to you, hail to . . . . . . O ye [people (?)], who are upon this land, I have said to you . . . ." Fragment 1ᴰ mentions "my portable statue which is in . . . ."

2 gives the titles of Takelot II.

3. Funereal formula pronounced by the Osiris Hapimen. Roman period.

13. Exhortation to various priests to utter a prayer for the ⌷𓏺⌷, Inhor (?). Roman period.

Pl. xxv. Stele of "the divine father of Osiris, the *aden*-officer, Horpanefer," and his wife, "the singer of Osiris, Taubenu." In the second register: "the . . . . . of Osiris, the *uab*-priest, Kari (?)," with his sister (i.e. wife), "the singer of Osiris Tanehasi"; and three

others. The third register names the father of Taubenu, "the scribe Hora." XXth (?) Dynasty.

On the right, inscription from the coffin of "the ⌷𓏺⌷, priest of Osiris Upshadtaui, priest of Horus, avenger of his father, priest of Isis the great, the mother of the god, priest of Horus, Buto, and Sekhmet, Imhotep." His father was "the ⌷𓏺⌷ and priest of Osiris, Horkheb"; his mother, "the sistrum-player of Khenti Amentiu, Dersh." Ptolemaic.

Pl. xxvii.-xxviii. Religious inscriptions from the tomb of the *uab*-priest Hordauankh. EAST WALL, ll. 1-8, Hymn to Osiris. Ll. 50-9 (numbered backwards), the Negative Confession, chapter 125 of the Book of the Dead. Ll. 51-55, praise of Osiris. NORTH WALL, cf. the photograph, pl. xxviii. 1, Hordauankh praises Osiris: in place of the usual altar, the four children of Horus are represented standing on a lotus flower. WEST WALL, speeches of Osiris and Thoth. XXth (?) Dynasty.

Pl. xxix. 1. Portion of a stele of the Middle Kingdom, narrating the merits of one Khety. The meaning is rendered obscure by lexicographical difficulties, even where the text is not defective. The following rendering is purely tentative :—

"(1) . . . . praised . . . . (2) . . . . . . road in his mission. Now when he knoweth . . . . (3) . . . . south to Aaaru-n-maset, north to Shath . . . . (4) . . . . in order to take away robbery, by bringing to silence: not cursing, nor striking with the stick . . . . (5) . . . . . I heard (?) . . . . (6) . . . . . . servant of love, spreading the love of his lord. It is what happens . . . . (7) . . . . in the . . . . . . nome, as chief of the districts. Speaking concerning . . . . (8) his lord. Entering in unto his lord, without being announced. His own word announces concerning that which he has brought to a prosperous issue . . . . (9) his lord.

Knowing that which is said beside lords. Free from evasion before the Qenbet. Armoured of heart because of [his] innocence (?) . . . . (10)·. . . . . for whom I had created boundaries, even as a knowing follower does (?) . . . . (11) Whose word his lord receiveth. Speaking a word because of its truth. Free from hindering (?) [1] his lord. Not robbing, nor (12) stealing his property. I did not . . . .[2] in the nome whence I went forth (?). I did not lust after (?) the wife of a man.[3] Nor did I covet her whom the poor man loved. (13) Verily, the son of a great man[4] who doeth so, his father repudiates him in the Qenbet. I did not receive the goods (14) of the wrongdoer (?).[5] I received him who made supplication to me. It is what the god loveth upon earth. I swear with my mouth . . . . . . (15) Khety, deceased. May life be united with every limb (?) of his, may he succeed . . . . (16) All that which I have said upon this [stele], it is truth . . . ." Here the fragment comes to an abrupt end.

5. Inscription from an ostrakon, in cursive hieroglyphs. " The hereditary prince, great in his dignity, great in his rank. Chief, hereditary prince, great in [his] dignity, ..." With these ordinary titles, the scribe apparently wished merely to test his reed. Roman period.

75. Pl. lii. The texts hitherto discussed have not been deficient in points of interest,

but they shrink into insignificance beside the monument to which we must now turn our attention. The great stele of Aahmes I belongs to the extensive category of building inscriptions. It is, however, distinguished from other specimens of the class by a dramatic style of composition, and by valuable historical information, which entitle it to a place among the most important documents yet rescued from the soil of Egypt.

In dignified narrative style, from which the usual bombast of official records is conspicuously absent, it is told how Aahmes sat with his spouse, the Queen Nefertari, within a chamber of his palace, conversing of the honours due to the dead. The questions of the queen lead Pharaoh to unfold his purpose. It is his grandmother Teta-shera who is the object of his solicitude; hitherto she has possessed no adequate place of worship in Abydos. For her therefore he will now build a pyramid and a chapel, endowed with lands and cattle and a priesthood. Scarcely has Pharaoh done speaking, and the edifice is already complete. After another picture of Aahmes reciting, with pious gesture, the habitual prayers, the inscription comes to an end.

Unusually picturesque as this narrative appears, it is but the variation of a common type of commemorative texts.[6] After a formal introduction, consisting of the date and the royal titles, the king is described as sitting among his courtiers, " counselling with his heart," " seeking the welfare " of this or that god, to whom he will fain erect a monument. The courtiers approve the plan with expressions of deferential praise. The remainder of such inscriptions deals with the details of the constructions, together with a few phrases lauding the wisdom of him who devised them. Here

---

[1] [glyph] , transitive, not found elsewhere.

[2] For the word, cf. *Pap. Prisse*, 14, 5.

[3] [glyph] is probably the [glyph] of the *Pap. Prisse*, in one obscure passage of which (ix. 13) the word is used apparently in a similar context [glyph] is found too in the Negative Confession, as Prof. ERMAN reminds me.

[4] [glyph] occurs in various passages, probably in the sense of " son of a great man ": cf. LANGE, *Sitzb. d. Kön. Pr. Akad. d. Wiss.* 1903, p. 603. As Prof. ERMAN observes, there is possibly an antithesis with the " poor man " of the previous sentence.

[5] i.e. as bribe (?).

[6] Perhaps the only two earlier examples are the stele of Neferhotep, found at Abydos by Mariette ; and the stele of Rahotep, PETRIE, *Koptos*, 12, 3.

the part of the courtiers is played by Queen Aahmes Nefertari, and. the god is replaced by Teta-shera. Both variations strike the note of the period: the XVIIIth Dynasty is the age of great Egyptian Queens.

Teta-shera was known to us from two sources, a wonderful statuette in the British Museum,[1] and a fragment of papyrus preserved at Gizeh,[2] where she is named together with the princess Satkames. Her relationship to Aahmes I is revealed for the first time by our stele: according to this she was at once the mother of his mother, and the mother of his father. Hence the parents of Aahmes were brother and sister. Further, if the stele rightly attributes to Teta-shera the title "great wife of a king," the grandfather of Aahmes will have been a Pharaoh of the XVIIth Dynasty. The difficult genealogical problems of the period are complicated still further by this new evidence, and their solution may best be left to the historian. A fact that seems to follow from the mention of Satkames[3] together with Teta-shera, may here be noted: the Pharaoh Kames must be relegated to at least the second generation before Aahmes.

The buildings in which Mr. CURRELLY discovered our stele are doubtless the remains of "the pyramid and chapel" dedicated by Aahmes to the memory of his grandmother: it will be interesting to learn what manner of constructions could thus be designated at this period. The Sacred Land, where they are said to have been situated, was part of the Abydene necropolis, as we are expressly informed by the stele of king Neferhotep recently published by Mr. MACE. From the sentence which immediately precedes the mention of this cenotaph, it would appear that the actual burial-place of Teta-shera—her tomb-chamber (...)—was at Thebes, where most of the princesses of that time were interred: and that she further owned a sepulchre (...) in the Thinite nome, i.e. probably at Abydos. These facts are, however, very obscurely expressed and the sequence of thought in the narration concealed by the absence of conjunctions. Perhaps the best way to render the passage clear will be to reproduce the translation, inserting in italics such words as are needful to convey the sense to the modern reader. "*Although* her chamber and her sepulchre are at this present time upon the soil of the Theban and the Thinite nomes *respectively, yet* this have I said unto thee, *for* my Majesty hath desired to let make for her *also* a pyramid and a chapel in the Sacred Land." It is, nevertheless, strange that Aahmes should have thought it needful to erect a pyramid and chapel for Teta-shera at Abydos, if she already possessed a sepulchre—whatever that may mean—in that locality.[4]

76. We may now turn to the stele itself. The scenes above the text show Aahmes in the act of offering to Teta-shera, and form an apt illustration of the last sentences of the text. The picture is represented in duplicate, for reasons of symmetry. The reversing of the figures has caused some change in the position of the arms, otherwise there is but little variation in treatment. As usual, the winged disk symbolizing the Horus " of Edfu, the great god," hovers overhead.

---

[1] No. 22, 558. A good photograph, BUDGE, *History IV.* p. 64. On the statuette, Teta-shera is only "king's mother." On the stele she bears the further title, "great wife of the king." These facts should be considered in connection with the theory of Prof. SETHE, who has sought to show (*Untersuchungen I.* p. 2) that where a princess is named "king's mother" without further title, she may be presumed to be the wife of a private man.

[2] cf. ERMAN, *Ä. Z.* xxxviii. (1900) p. 150.

[3] Her name implies that she was the daughter of Kames.

---

[4] This difficulty at first led me to suggest another rendering: that here given I owe to Prof. BREASTED.

TRANSLATION.

"Now it came to pass that his Majesty sat in the *zadu*-hall,[1] even the king of Upper and Lower Egypt, Nebpehtira, the son of Ra, Aahmes, gifted with life, and the princess, great of favours, great of charm, the king's daughter, the king's sister, wife of the god, great wife of the king, Aahmes Nefertari, who liveth, was in the presence of his Majesty. And the one spoke unto the other, seeking the welfare of the departed dead[2]; (which is) the pouring of water, the making of oblations upon the altar, and the enriching of the stele at the beginning of every season, at the feast of the New Moon,[3] at the feast of the Month, the feast of the going forth of the *Sem*-priest,[4] the feast (called) Ceremonies of the Night, (which is) the feast of the 5th day, the feast of the 6th day, the feast of Hak<er>, the feast of Uag, the feast of Thoth, and the beginning of every season of heaven and of earth.

"Then spoke his sister, she made answer unto him. 'Wherefore have these things been recalled? To what end hath this matter been related? What (thought) is come to thy heart?'

"The king himself, he said to her, 'I, even I, have bethought me of the mother of my mother,

the mother of my father, the great wife of the king, the mother of the king, Teta-shera, the deceased. Her chamber and her sepulchre are at this present time upon the soil of the Theban and the Thinite nomes.[5] This have I said unto thee, for my Majesty hath desired to let make for her a pyramid and a chapel in the Sacred Land, as a memorial-presentation of my Majesty[6]; its lake being dug, its trees being planted, and its offerings being instituted; equipped with people, furnished[7] with lands. endowed with cattle; *ka*-priests and lectors (engaged) in their duties, every man knowing his instructions.'

"While yet his Majesty spoke this word, these buildings were carried out with good speed.[8] His Majesty did this, inasmuch as he loved her beyond anything. Never[9] had the ancestral kings performed the like thereof for their mothers. Then his Majesty thrust forth his arm, and bent his hand, and made for her a Royal Oblation, and an oblation of Geb, and the [greater][10] ennead, and the lesser ennead . . . . and of [Anubis] in the Divine Booth, thousands of bread, beer, oxen, geese, *aua*-cattle . . . . [for the Queen Teta-shera.]"

---

[1] A hall of the palace; we often read of Pharaoh as sitting there with his courtiers.

[2] "Those yonder," a periphrasis for the dead. ⌐ᴧ⌐ is written for ᴧᴧᴧ, from the hieratic stroke with the point above it.

[3] ▢ ᴧᴧᴧ gives for the first time the reading of the feast usually written ⊖ ⊂⊃.

[4] Celebrated on the 4th day of the month.

[5] This obscure sentence can hardly be translated otherwise: its meaning has been discussed above.

[6] Lit: "with the presenting (?) of monuments of my Majesty." The expression appears very unusual.

[7] Lit: "yoked."

[8] This is a paraphrase. I have to thank Professor ERMAN for what is doubtless the correct literal translation of the words:—"Behold, his Majesty spoke this word, while these things were built with action."

[9] ᴧᴧᴧ ▢⊚ for ⌐ᴧ⌐ ▢⊚ .

[10] ⌠ doubtless omitted.

CHAPTER VIII.

DESCRIPTION OF PLATES.

77. Pl. i. 1-10. Worked slate of the Ist Dynasty and earlier; from the lowest deposits of the early town, within the walls of the Osiris Temenos. No. 1 has a curious ribbed pattern upon it. The palettes, No. 2 and 3, are ornamented round the edge in the usual way of late prehistoric times; Nos. 8-10 are carefully and regularly made, while Nos. 4, 5, 7 are quite rough. No. 4 has been worn through by constant use; No. 9 has some marks upon it. No. 11 is a polished quartzose axe-head of the Ist Dynasty. No. 12 is a glazed quartz pendant of the Ist Dynasty, broken at the bottom; fragments of similar pendants were found. No. 13 is a ring of slate of the Ist Dynasty, the use of which is unknown. Several similar objects, chiefly of pottery, were found during the excavations. No. 14 is the fragment of a marble vase from the early town. No. 15, a stele of the Ist Dynasty, like those found round the tombs of Mersekha and Qa (cf. *R. T.* i, pls. xxxv and xxxvi). From the fact that it is the only other Ist Dynasty object found in this part of the cemetery, it is probably the stele belonging to the rifled tomb μ 22, situated slightly to the north of the south-east gate of the Middle Fort. The other objects from this tomb were, a perfect ivory draughtsman of the type found in the tomb of Zer (*R. T.* ii, xxxv, 5), and various fragments of slate and alabaster vases, from which the original shapes have been restored (see below, pl. xxxi).

78. Pl. ii-iv. Flint knives from the lower levels of the Temple of Osiris, except No. 4, which is from the Temple of Aahmes I. The numerals placed at the bottom right-hand corner of each refer to the levels at which they were found above an arbitrary datum (see *Abydos* II). No. 26 is of a shape hitherto unknown.

Pl. v, No. 1. A view of the Shunet-ez-zebib looking north. On the west (left hand) may be seen the small outer wall, showing above the sand. The large opening to the south marks the original position of the south gate.

The small opening in the northern wall is the result of a Coptic attempt to form a house by hollowing out the brickwork. In the extreme left of the photograph a mound of rubbish is noticeable. Within three yards of this was the tomb μ 50 (see below). An upward curve visible on the brickwork shows the height of the sand, before disturbed by Maspero in examining the walls. Below this the pilasters are faintly visible. No. 2 is a photograph of the Coptic Deir or monastery looking west. The ancient wall may be distinguished from the modern, in the south, by its darker and more weathered appearance.

No. 3. On the left is visible the opening caused by the falling in of the western gate. The north gateway is also visible, and the elaborate courts through which one enters may be made out. The level of the sand against the north wall before excavating can also be seen. No. 4. The east wall of the Shuneh after excavation, showing the damage done by the Copts in undermining the western side, and thus causing the wall to collapse. The pilasters and false doorways can be distinctly seen, with the stucco still adhering to the greater part.

No. 5. The west trench was not excavated

by Maspero, and the strata of rubbish and fallen brick can be distinguished in the photograph. No. 6. A burial in a *magur*. The pot has been removed from its original place, beneath the foundations of the wall, and turned on its side to show the method of placing the skeleton. Originally it was mouth downwards over the body. It belongs to the earlier part of the IInd Dynasty, as shown by the pottery buried with it.

79. Pl. vi.-viii. The plans have been described in the text of the first chapter.

Pl. ix.-x. Those sealings which are marked μ were found in the Middle Fort, whilst the mark ʊ shows those that were discovered in the Shuneh. Nos. 1 and 2 are similar to those found in the Royal Tombs (see *R. T.* i, 184, 185.) No. 3 is the sealing of an unknown king, Sekhem-abt Per-en-maat. The name resembles that of Perabsen (see *R. T.* ii, pl. xxi.). The Horus-name Sekhem-abt, and the Set-name Per-en-maat are combined. On a sealing of Perabsen in Professor Petrie's collection the two names are combined in the same way (c.f. PETRIE, *Hist.* vol. i, fig. 17, B.) He is possibly to be placed between Perabsen and Khasekhemui.

The greater number of the sealings were found in the Middle Fort and are marked μ. No. 9 is a sealing of Khasekhemui, last king of the IInd Dynasty. These are all dealt with by Mr. A. H. Gardiner in the chapter on the inscriptions.

Nos. 28-42 are scratchings made with a sharpened piece of wood or reed on the clay caps of the jars.

80. Pl. xi., Nos. 1-3. No. 1 is a small scarab of green glaze with a circular pattern. In the same grave was found a steatite button (No. 2) cut with the hieroglyph *ankh* and a bordering line. A button of similar type of the VIth Dynasty was found by Mr. Mace at Abydos in 1900. The button is square in shape and is of the same design (see *El Amrah and Abydos*, pl. xl, 1). No. 3 is of glazed steatite with a

more usual pattern (see GARSTANG, *Mahásna*, pl. xxxix).

These are all from later burials in the courtyard of the Middle Fort.

No. 4-18. Contents of a XIIth Dynasty tomb, discovered in cemetery G. The objects were drawn by Mr. A. M. Blackman. Nos. 4-6 belong to the same necklace and are of amethyst. No. 5 of carnelian and No. 8 of amethyst were possibly threaded upon the same string. No. 7 consisted of amethyst and blue-green glazed beads, with a uzat-eye amulet of carnelian, all strung from a carnelian spacer pierced with ten holes. Nos. 9 and 11 are of blue glaze, and No. 10 of amethyst. These drawings of course only give specimen beads, but the full number were found for complete strings. Nos. 12-17 are alabasters of various shapes, and No. 18 is an ivory spoon. No. 19-26. The lower part of this plate is occupied by the contents of tomb μ 50 of the XIIth Dynasty. As will be seen on the general plan (pl. viii), this tomb lay slightly to the east of a small mastaba, to the west of the Shuneh. The section of the tomb is given on pl. xx, No. 7. It consisted of a straight shaft cut through the water-laid sand to a depth of 36 ft., and bricked in at the top to keep back the loose wind-driven sand. The four upper chambers had been originally rifled, but the two lower remained untouched. The two ears of stucco (No. 19) were all that remained of the coffin in the northern chamber. Of the kohl-pots, Nos. 23, 24, 26 were of alabaster and No. 25 was of green glaze. A mirror (as No. 20) was laid in front of each skeleton. In the northern chamber was a string of carnelian beads with a scarab inscribed, "The *Ka*-priest of Shenti" [a goddess Shenty was worshipped at Abydos (see CAULFIELD, *Temple of the Kings*, pl. ix)]; also a necklace of amethyst beads with an uninscribed scarab of the same material, and a beautifully worked amulet of glazed steatite with rounded back (No. 22) belonging to a necklace of the large green glazed beads usual in this period ; while near the ankles was a string of small white beads. In the southern chamber were found two necklaces of carnelian and amethyst and a necklace of green glazed beads, but no scarabs.

81. Pl. xii, 1, 2, 3, see section 18. No. 4, and 5, colossal granite head found in the upper levels of the Osiris Temple, 1901.

Pl. xiii. The great limestone stele reproduced on this plate was discovered in the Osiris Temenos, and is now in the possession of the Cairo Museum. It is a very important historical monument and gives the entire family of Queen Áu-het-ábu, presumably the mother of Sebek-hotep II, of Dynasty XIII. (see PETRIE, *Hist.* ii,

211.) In the first panel she is represented with the royal head-dress, seated before some offerings. She is here called "The Royal Mother Áu-het-ábu, born of (the lady) Senusert." The king's relations are omitted ; and the queen appears to have also married a commoner, as her two sons, Res-Ptah-ur and Nekhtà, and one daughter, Set-en-au-het-àbu, are not of royal descent. On the other hand, two daughters, Sebek-dedet and Mutà-sentà, are royal children, as well as her sons Sebek-hotep and Senb, who are known elsewhere. The lack of titles on the stele is an indication that the queen came of an unimportant family of the middle or lower classes. The genealogy appears to stand as follows :—

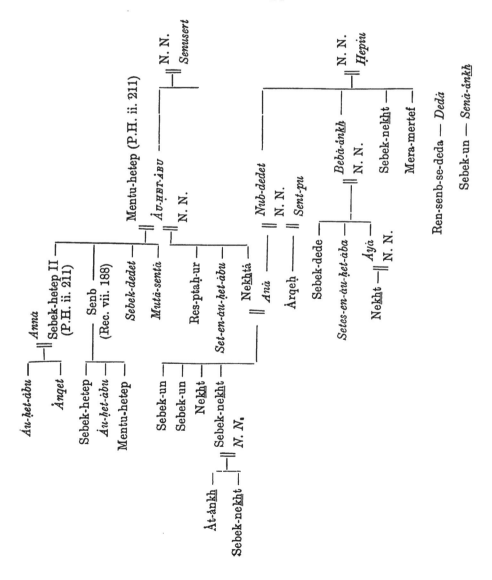

82. Pl. xiv. Stele of Ay, see section 20.

Pl. xv. No. 1, see section 20.

Nos. 2-7. Miscellaneous objects of the XIIth-XVIIIth Dynasties.

No. 2 is a slate palette of the XIIth Dynasty found in a tomb of that date in cemetery G. No. 3 is an inscription from a grey basalt statuette of the XIIIth Dynasty. No. 4 is an alabaster hollowed dish in the form of a fish, probably of the XVIIIth Dynasty. No. 5 is a fragment of a clay sealing of about the XIIth Dynasty. No. 6 is the inscription upon a fragment of a steatite statuette of the XIIth Dynasty, found in the Osiris Temenos. Nos. 8-10, scarabs from tomb, μ 18, a later burial in the Middle Fort of the XVIIIth Dynasty. From a rifled tomb comes No. 11, a beautifully worked scarab, engraved with a charm against fear.

No. 12. Type of six pairs of gold uraei found in a rifled tomb of Cemetery ν. The tails are fixed on separately behind. No. 13 is an ivory object of unknown use from a plundered tomb in the Middle Fort.

No. 14. A very fine ivory kohl-pot of the XVIIIth Dynasty. (A photograph is on pl. xvi, No. 2.) The side shown in the drawing is convex, that in the photograph is slightly concave. It will be seen that on the side shown in the photograph are the remains of three pins. A similar triple kohl-pot is shown on pl. xlvi of *El Amrah and Abydos*, and pl. xxi of *El Arabeh*.[1]

---

[1] *Note on the method of carrying the kohl-pot.*—In the Cairo Museum, Salle N-T, there is the lower part of an XVIIIth Dynasty quartzite-sandstone statuette, belonging to the [hieroglyphs], Hereditary prince Aahmes, and suspended from his waist-belt by ornamented strings is a three-cylinder kohl-pot. When cataloguing the *fayence*-vases in the Cairo Museum, Baron Von Bissing observed that *kohl*-pots of this type often had small holes drilled along the top edge between the cylinders; and in a foot-note on page 85 of his *Fayencegefasse* [*Cat. Gén. Mus., Cairo*, 1902], he points out that these holes may be for fastening on a lid to the pots. The statuette of Aahmes, however, shows that they were made for the purpose of hanging the pot to the belt, either by passing

83. Nos. 15-19. These objects, with the three pottery vases, figured on pl. xxxiii (Nos. 33, 35, 36), were from a tomb dated to the reign of Akhenaten, by the scarab on pl. xxi, 2. It was in the Middle Fort, and the plan and section are given on pl. xx 9. On pl. xvi, 7; xxi, 2; are shown photographs of objects from this tomb. No. 15 is a vase of a fine buff ware, with whitened surface and is of a peculiar shape. Traces of degenerated handles may be seen in the knobs on the shoulders. No. 16, a vase in the shape of a pomegranate of a fine yellowish ware (see pl. xvi, 6, and *El Amrah and Abydos*, pl. lv, 19). No. 17 is a pectoral of green glaze, with figures and lines raised in black. The holes in the back are so arranged that the string will not show obtrusively from the front. No. 18, an amulet of blue-green glaze, in the form of two ducks placed side by side; this originally served as a connector for two strings of beads. No. 19, a green-glazed cone-bead of peculiar shape. Turning to the photograph (xvi, 7), the two small green-glaze kittens are types from a necklace of blue beads alternating with these animals. The two pairs of black pottery studs were probably used as earrings. The same form of large disc may be seen in the figures above (Nos. 3 and 5), of the Graeco-Egyptian figure-vases.

84. Pl. xvi, 1. Ivory handle of a tray or spoon from a plundered tomb in cemetery ν.

No. 2. This has already been described with the drawing (pl. xv, 14).

Nos. 3-5. These were all objects from the grave of a girl, not more than fourteen years of age, buried in the south-east corner of the Shuneh. The coffin had been an oblong box, but was quite decayed. The tall standing figure

---

the strings through them, or by inserting pegs into them, to which the strings were attached. Sometimes one side of the object is flat or slightly curved, and this is now seen to have been done in order that the pot might rest against the body.—A. E. P. W.

E

(No. 3) was of finely-polished orange pottery, with black hair. The mouth of the vase is on her head, and resting on the arm is a pottery casket, the lid movable on a pivot. The clay, the colouring, the motive of the figure-vase, and the casket are Aegean in source; while the wig and earrings are Egyptian. The vase next to it was of a rough but well modelled pottery, coloured with a representation of a drake with bright plumage, on a white ground, surrounded by semicircular lines of different colours. This is purely Egyptian of the late XVIIIth Dynasty.

No. 4 is a ring vase, with lotus flowers, buds, and pomegranates placed around the top; made of orange-coloured clay, streaked with dark red lines. This type is purely Aegean, and is evidently made of clay imported from the other side of the Mediterranean. No. 5. This seated figure shows its Aegean source very clearly. The upper part of a figure, of exactly similar shape and material, was found at Abydos by Mr. Mace in 1900 (*El Amrah and Abydos*, pl. xlviii). No. 7. This group has been dealt with in connection with the drawings on pl. xv (15-19).

85. Pl. xvii. A XIIth Dynasty brick shaft, 10½ ft. by about 8, was being cleared, when about 5 ft. from the surface a tomb was found, let in to the south side, and filling most of the shaft (see pl. xx, 8). It had a brick wall around the exposed sides, and was covered by limestone slabs and brickwork. The coffin was of black wood, with yellow ornamentation, but it had fallen to pieces. The eyes on the coffin, and also on the pulverized cartonnage, were inlaid, and the face and hands were covered with base gold leaf. The mummy, also decayed, was that of a woman, and upon the ushabtis laid by her side, her name seems to have been *Neb* . . . . . The coffin was resting on three limestone blocks, evidently taken from neighbouring tombs of the early XVIIIth Dynasty. After the clearance of the tomb, the

shaft was emptied to the bottom, where only some bones and a stele were found. The latter will be published later. The contents of the above-mentioned tomb were very rich, and the objects numbered 2, 13, and 20 may be seen at the Ashmolean Museum, Oxford, the rest being in the Cairo Museum. No. 1 is a pottery bottle, of which form a smaller one was also found. No. 2 is a heavy gold ring inscribed with the name of Isis; No. 3 is a silver ring set with a blue glass frog; and Nos. 4 and 5 are silver scarab. rings. No. 6 is an ivory ear-stud. No. 7 are two of the seven ushabtis found. They are of black painted wood, inscribed in yellow. No. 8 are inlaid eyes of the usual kind, from the coffin and cartonnage. No. 9 is a pair of ivory ear-plugs, which were worn forced through the lobe of the ear. The mirror (No. 10) is of bronze, and has a plain wooden handle in perfect preservation. Several tortoise-shell bracelets (No. 11) were found. Of the two combs (No. 12) the first is made of ivory, the second of wood. No. 13 is a very beautiful ivory dish. No. 14 is a blue and black glazed kohl-pot, belonging to which are the two wooden sticks (No. 17). No. 15 is a shark's-tooth amulet, probably from the Red Sea; No. 16 a red glazed pottery disk; No. 18 a bronze ladle; and No. 19 two unknown objects of wood with ivory studs on them. No. 20 is a pilgrim bottle with hinged lid, made of pure tin. [For use of tin in Egypt, see Dr. GLADSTONE, in *P.S.B.A.* xiv, p. 223.] Besides these objects there was a large quantity of small coloured beads. Two of the inscribed limestone blocks upon which the coffin in this tomb was resting are shown on pl. xix. The first is inscribed with a *seten de ḥetep* formula for the *Kas* of "the Royal Scribe Kha-riy," and "the Royal Scribe, Amen-em-ḥeb." The second gives a similar prayer for the *Ka* of "The Captain of the Great Guard of the Dewey Aten, Ka-riåa." The "Dewey Aten" is the name of the *daha-byeh* of Akhenaten, but it is here, perhaps, the name of a troop of soldiers. [*A.Z.* xxxix, p. 63 and 66]. The same man is mentioned in MARIETTE, *Cat. Ab.*, 1062.

86. Pl. xviii. Objects from later burials in the Middle Fort:—(No. 1) A heart amulet roughly carved in schist, with the knob at the top pierced for suspension. In the same grave was found a scarab (No. 2) of the Hyksos period. This was perhaps an heirloom, since the beads in the grave belonged to the XVIIIth Dynasty. (No. 4) scarab inscribed with the name of Thothmes III. The burial was that of a still-born infant. The coffin was made by hollowing out a piece of a palm trunk, in which the child was then placed for burial. (No. 5) A small ivory kohl-pot, inlaid with black, and with a lid of ebony. The cover is kept in place by a slender ivory pin, which was also used for the kohl-stick. (No. 3) A large shabti of quartzite sandstone, now in the Cairo Museum. This was found in the rubbish of the south-west corner of the Shuneh. The inscription is dealt with in the chapter on the inscriptions. From it we learn that the figure belonged to Amenemheb, the "governor of the two granaries," the son of Tehuti and Nes-nub. A photograph of this figure was published in *Abydos* II (xxxii, 10).

Nos. 6-12. Contents of a tomb probably of the XIXth Dynasty. The shabtis (as No. 6), and shabti jar (No. 12) bear the name of the "Osirian, the singer of Isis, Pa-nefu." [For the title and office of singer, see ERMAN, *Aegypten*, vol. 2, pp. 399-401.] An ivory object (No. 7) was found near the skull. This is probably an ear-stud or something similar (see pl. xvi, 7 and text). A copper ring engraved with the signs:— "Horus, lord of heaven," was found near the right hand. No. 9 is half of an alabaster ear-stud, the corresponding part having a small spike to fit into the central tube (see *Ermitage Cat.*, p. 313, No. 2,189). No. 11 is a dish of alabaster, in the shape of a fish.

Pl. xix, 1A-1D. Drawings of four sides of an obelisk from the Osiris Temple. (No. 2)

Jamb of the tomb of Tetathy, found re-used in the cemetery. Nos. 3 and 4 are XVIIIth Dynasty jambs of tombs which were re-used as supports for a coffin of the same date in Cemetery G (see pl. xvii and text).

87. Pl. xx, 1-3. These are burials of the VIth Dynasty, contracted and lying with head to the north. The pottery vase from No. 1 is of the type of No. 24 (pl. xxxii). The vases in No. 2 belong to type 11, whilst those of No. 3 belong to types 23-26.

Nos. 4 and 5 belong to the XIth Dynasty, and are the latest contracted burials known. The other tombs have been described above; No. 6 in sect. 18. No. 7 is described in. sect. 80. No. 8 in sect. 85. No. 9 in sect. 83.

Pl. xxi, 1, Slabs of Aahmes I of white limestone, with figure of Osiris, from the Osiris Temple. These had been re-used as part of a foundation by the kings of the XXVIth Dynasty. (No. 2) A group of small objects from tomb μ 26 (see sect. 83). In the middle is an eye of coloured glass inlaid in gold. On the right is a scarab engraved with a sphinx, and the cartouche of Akhenaten. The long pendant beads are of coloured pottery. (No. 3) A finely worked ibis-head of bronze with an inlaid eye of green glass. This was found in the western trench of the Shuneh, to the south of the gateway, and belongs probably to the XXIInd Dynasty. In the same region were found three solid bronze fishes of the same date.

88. Pl. xxii. Shabti jars from Cemetery ν, with the lids in the shape of a jackal's head. The inscriptions are noticed below (chap. xli). A large number of these vases were found in 1901 (see MACIVER and MACE, *El Amrah and Abydos*, pl. lvi).

Pl. xxiii, 1-3. A shabti pot and group of all the types of shabtis from Cemeteries μ and ν. A drawing of the jar is given on pl. xxii, 2; and a shabti from the same burial as that on the extreme right of No. 3, is drawn on pl. xviii, 6. No. 4. These photographs show

some of the general types of pottery vases in
which the mummied ibises were buried (see
pls. xxxiv and xxxv). No. 5 is the lid of
an infant's coffin, made of coarse clay, such as
were found by Mariette in the southern trench
of the Shuneh (cf. pl. xxviii, 5 and 6).

Pl. xxiv, 1A-1E are portions of engraved
ebony from a rifled tomb in Cemetery ν.
(No. 2) Inscription on the back of a statuette of
Tekeloth I. (No. 3) Inscription on the footcase
of the cartonnage of Hapi-men, a magnate
of the XXXth Dynasty (*Ab. I.* lxxix, 9).

4-12. Objects in blue glaze from a foundation deposit of Rameses III. From the
Temple of Osiris.

13. Transcription on the four sides of a
small, headless, limestone crouching statue of
the XXXth Dynasty. From the upper levels
of the Osiris Temenos (1901-2).

Pl. xxv. Stele of Hor-pa-nefer and family,
who seem to have been Sudanis; from the
Osiris Temenos. Inscription from lid of coffin of
Imhotep, see *Abydos* I, lxxix, 6.

Pl. xxvi. Scenes in the tomb of Hor-dedu-
ankh, painted in black line on white stucco.
The roof of the tomb could not be copied, as
it had fallen in.

Pl. xxvii. Inscription round the scenes in
the tomb of Hor-dedu-ankh, of the XXIInd
Dynasty (see Chap. on inscriptions).

89. Pl. xxviii, 1. Photograph of the north
wall of the painted tomb of Hor-dedu-
ankh. The deceased is shown invoking Osiris;
above this is the boat of the sun. (No. 2) A
small head in white limestone from Cemetery ν.
From the strong resemblance to a portrait
published by SCHÄFER, it seems probable that
this may represent Psammetichus I (cf. *Ä. Z.*
xxxiii, p. 116).

3. A piece of mud used for sealing a roll of
papyri, scratched with a pointed instrument.
Probably of the XXXth Dynasty. Found in
the rubbish of the south end of the Shuneh.

4. Head of Nekht-hor-heb from the side of

a seated figure of a goddess dedicated by him;
now in Cairo Museum (*Abydos* I, lxx, 12).

5 and 6. Lids of coffins from infant burials.
No. 6 is decorated with a figure of the god Bes
(see pl. xxiii, 5). These were found in the
south of the Shuneh. No. 7, a limestone
statuette of the Ptolemaic period, covered with
gold leaf and having the eyes inlaid with
coloured glass (Cairo Museum).

Pl. xxix, 1. Inscribed slab of limestone
from the Osiris Temenos. The name of the
person is unfortunately lost. (No. 2) A scarab
from the rubbish of the Middle Fort. (No. 3) is
the mummy label of wood for "Demetrius, son
of Serapias," of the Roman period. (No. 4)
Amulet of the *Ka* made of greenish glaze,
XXVIth Dynasty. (No. 5) Inscription on an
ostrakon from the Temenos of Osiris.

Pl. xxx. A stele of the Ptolemaic period
from the upper levels of the Temple of Osiris,
containing the names of Hor-pa-Makheru, and
Anher, priest of Thoth.

Pl. xxxA. Inscription in black on an ibis
burial vase, consisting of account for oil and
corn. XXIInd-XXIVth Dynasty.

Pl. xxxi. Slate and alabaster bowls recon-
structed from fragments found in tomb μ 22 of
the Ist Dynasty (see sect. 77).

90. Pl. xxxii. In room C of the Middle
Fort were found a number of vases, which are
dated to the IInd Dynasty by the large pot
(No. 12) with which they were found. The
types of these pots are given. (Nos. 1, 2, and
12-16.)

Nos. 4 and 5 were found beneath the wall of
the Shuneh in the south-east corner (see text).

Nos. 6 and 7 were found in room A of
the Middle Fort.

No. 11 is from a burial of the VIth Dynasty
(see pl. xx, 2).

Nos. 18-21 were found against the west
wall of the courtyard of the Middle Fort, and
are probably of the VIth Dynasty. (Polished
red ware.)

Nos. 23-26, are from a contracted burial of the VIth-VIIth Dynasty (see pl. xx, 3).

Pl. xxxiii, 27-32, are of the XIth-XIIth Dynasty, and are all from burials in the Middle Fort.

33, 35, 36, are all from tomb μ 26 (cf. pl. xx. 9).

39-42 are also from the Middle Fort.

45-53 are from the Shuneh and Middle Fort.

Pls. xxxiv, xxxv. Types of pottery vases from the Ibis cemetery in the southern corner of the Shuneh.

No. 61 has an inscription in black across the top and is of whitened pottery. All these vases are probably of the XXIInd-XXVIth Dynasty.

91. Pls. xxxvi-xxxviii. Cf. text, Chapter II.

Pl. xxxix, 31-36. Fragments of alabaster dishes made in the form of a trussed duck. 33 and 36 show the open ends. 34 shows the other end, which was closed. 32 and 35 show the side. 37 is the top of what was probably a bowl with two handles for suspending it. These are seldom if ever found during any other period, and are made with the artistic finish and care so characteristic of the XIIth Dynasty.

Pl. xl, 1-11. This plate shows more of these dishes. 4 and 7 are drawings of the inside of the fragment.

14 is a fragment of the so-called pan-grave pottery. It is brown in colour and covered with incised lines. This fragment was left by the first plunderers.

15 is an inscribed fragment of Roman red pottery, IVth cent., A.D. This was left by the second plunderers.

16. A scale drawing of the granite sarcophagus in the tomb of Senusert III.

19. Gaming board for a game like draughts, found in the sand at the top of the shaft descending to the tomb of Senusert III. The marks in the spaces are probably connected with the game.

Pl. xli. The plan of the tomb of Senusert III.

Pl. xlii. Views of the tomb of Senusert III.

92. Pl. xliii, 1, shows a view of the end of the pole-roof chamber; the two men are seated on the piles of rubbish with which it was nearly filled. Above the one to the right is the hole smashed through the ceiling in order to reach the passage on the level above.

2 is a view of the first granite plug from the plugged passage. This is the one that was dropped into the room by digging under it.

3 gives a view of some of the walls and passages in the Aahmes town. The dark shadow in the centre falls across I of house 1. The streak of light that divides the shadow is the door into room D of house 1.

Pl. xliv, 1-5. Forms restored from fragments found in the tomb of Senusert III.

The forms from the Aahmes town are likewise restored from fragments.

Pl. xlv, 1, shows the entrance A and the gate into B. The sloping way C can also be seen. The gateway to the right is the one from B 1 into the first terrace. 2, in front of which the Abadi boy is standing, shows how the bricks of the lower part of the wall are less worn than those higher up. This was no doubt due to the banking up of sand against the lower part of the wall.

3 gives a very good idea of how the pots of the corner deposit lay.

4 is the north end of the second wall and the north side of the brick wall.

5 is taken from the room G, and shows the sloping ascent and the men at work on the first terrace.

93. Pl. xlvi. These are the forms of alabaster and painted limestone model vases found in the deposit at the corner of the terrace temple.

Pl. xlvii. The upper part of this continues the model vases. 67 is a model mace-head in limestone. 68-105 are the pottery forms; 104 and 105 are drawn 1 : 6.

Pl. xlviii, 16, shows the form of the band of gold found with the deposit. 1-15 show the designs on the fragments of blue glazed pottery that were found in the town. The blue was particularly good and had the soft turquoise shade.

17 shows one of the deposits of paddles and sticks in the position in which they were found.

18 is a potsherd on which some workman has drawn two serpents.

19, a fragment of moulding, perhaps from an altar cornice, or some other ornamental part of the building.

Pl. xlix. Plan of the tomb of Aahmes I.

Pl. l, 1 and 2, are views of the stele of Queen Teta-shera.

3 and 5 are side and front views of the statuette found in the Aahmes cemetery.

4 and 6 are side and front views of the figure of Renut found in the shrine of Queen Teta-shera.

7 shows Ta-Urt with a woman within her protecting arm. This was from the town of Aahmes.

8 is the ushabti figure of Pa-ari, the keeper of the pyramid of Aahmes I temple. This is of white limestone, painted and then covered with pitch.

9 is a broken ushabti of limestone, found in the same cemetery.

10. This gives a view of the entrance into the tomb of Aahmes I.

Pl. li. Plan of shrine of Queen Teta-shera.

Pl. lii. Stele of Queen Teta-shera.

Pl. liii. Plan of terrace temple and town.

94. Pl. liv. Inscription from a rough piece of limestone, found in the builders' town of Aahmes I. The text is commented upon by Professor Spiegelberg. (See § 69.)

Pl. lv. The same in hieroglyphic characters.

Pl. lvi. Photographs of the builders' town of Aahmes I.

Pl. lvii. Various small objects from the town of Aahmes I.

Pl. lviii, 1-5, show fragments of the flat thick yellow dishes that were supposed not to continue beyond the XIIth Dynasty. The ornament is incised.

6-7 are two examples of the black incised ware that was filled with white. This was already known in the XIIth Dynasty.

8, 9, 10 are fragments of the yellow pottery of the XVIIIth Dynasty ornamented with designs taken from Cypriote pottery.

11 is the neck of a false-necked vase. These were probably shipped over from Crete or Mycenae full of some merchandize.

12-20 show the dolls and children's animal toys found in the rooms of the Aahmes town.

21. An engraved limestone kohl-pot found in the Aahmes town.

23. This bronze knife was one of the very few scraps of bronze found in the town.

24. A pot-mark scratched in the unbaked clay.

Pl. lix, 1, 2, 3, 4, are kohl pots of the ordinary kind; but 5 and 6 being of blue marble show that this material was used as late as the XVIIIth Dynasty, and did not cease with the XIIth. Of course these may have come from earlier times or earlier graves.

12-15 were model vases, 13, 14 and 15 of the same kind as those found in the deposit.

Pl. lx. The pottery from the town.

Pl. lxi. Sketch map of the desert.

INDEX.

F

PRINTED BY GILBERT AND RIVINGTON LIMITED, ST. JOHN'S HOUSE, CLERKENWELL, E.C.

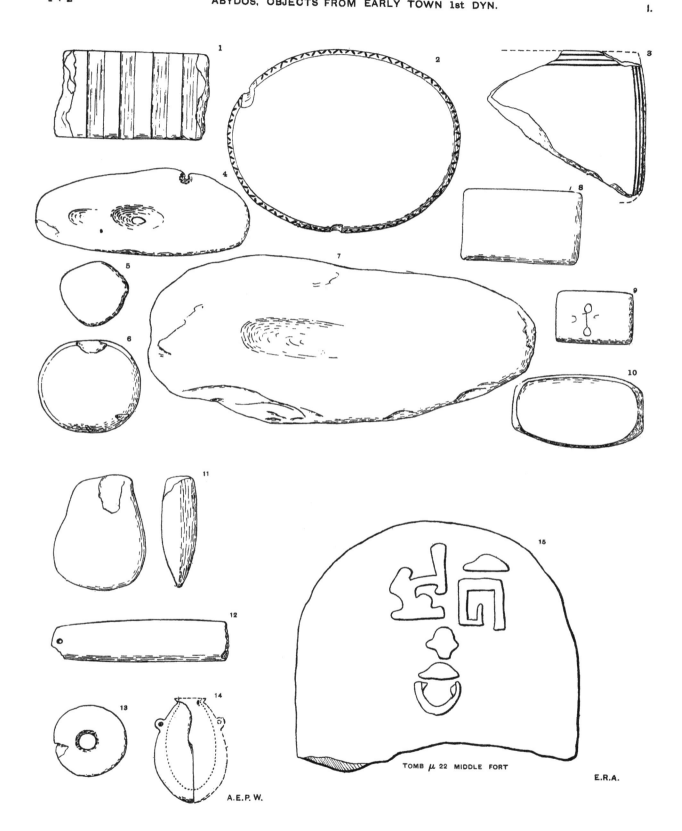

TOMB μ 22 MIDDLE FORT

A.E.P.W.

E.R.A.

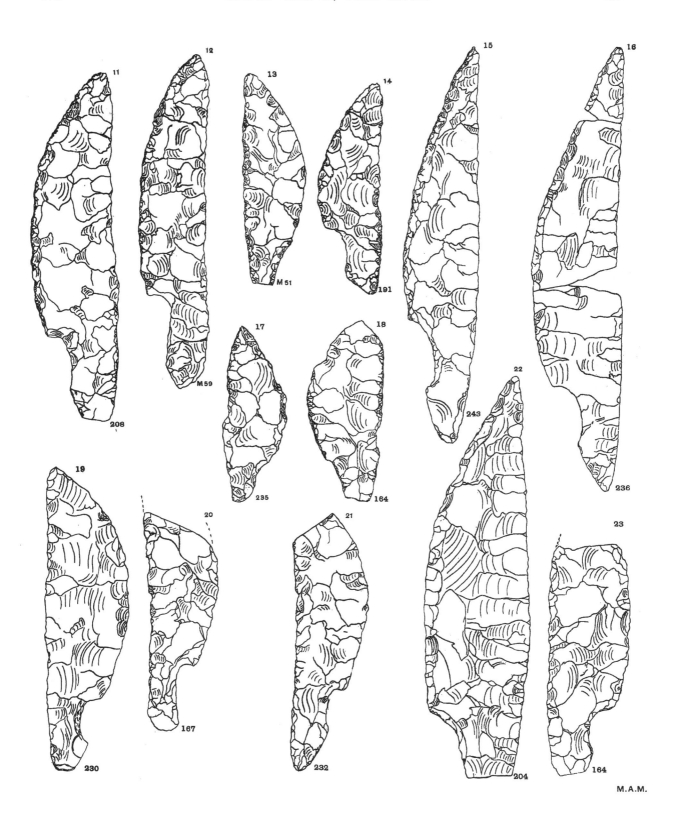

M.A.M.

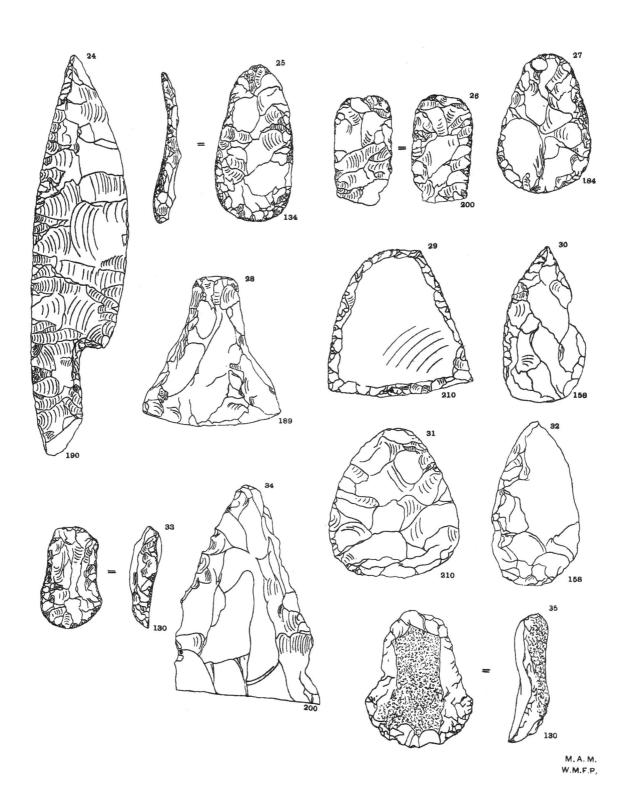

1 VIEW OF SHUNEH. LOOKING NORTH.

2. VIEW OF COPTIC DEIR. LOOKING WEST.

3. INTERIOR OF SHUNEH. LOOKING NORTH.

4. EAST WALL OF SHUNEH.

5. MEN WORKING IN WEST TRENCH OF SHUNEH.

6 EARLY BURIAL IN LARGE POT

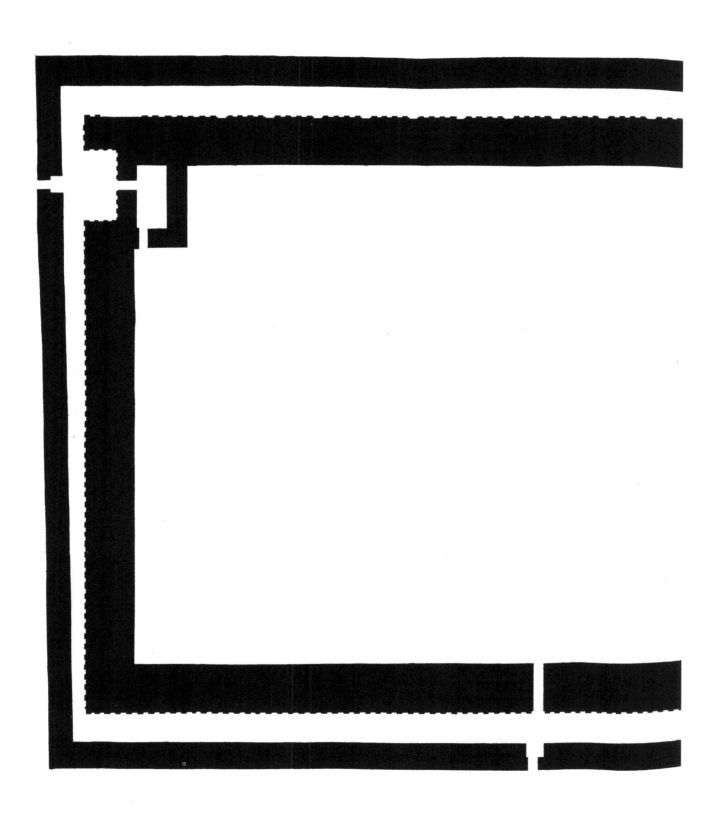

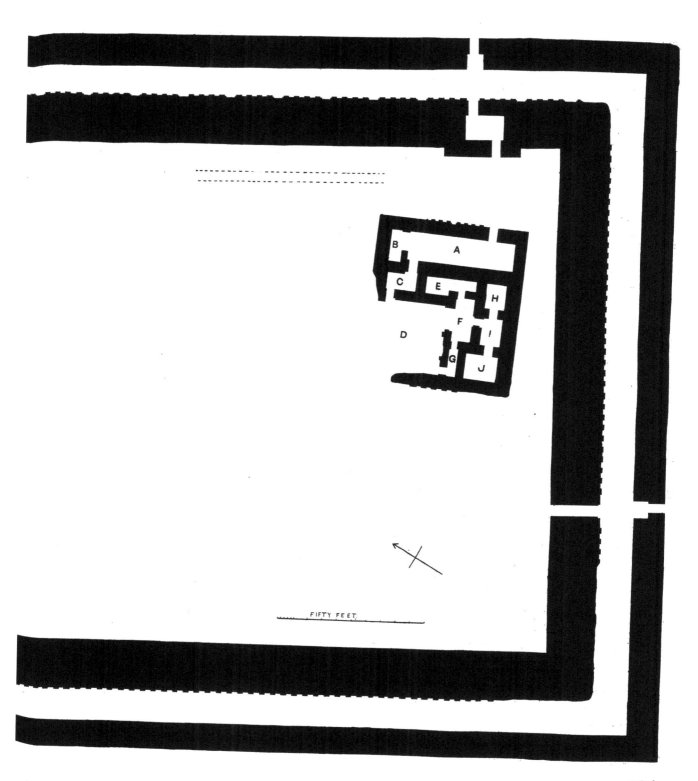

FIFTY FEET.

E.R.A.

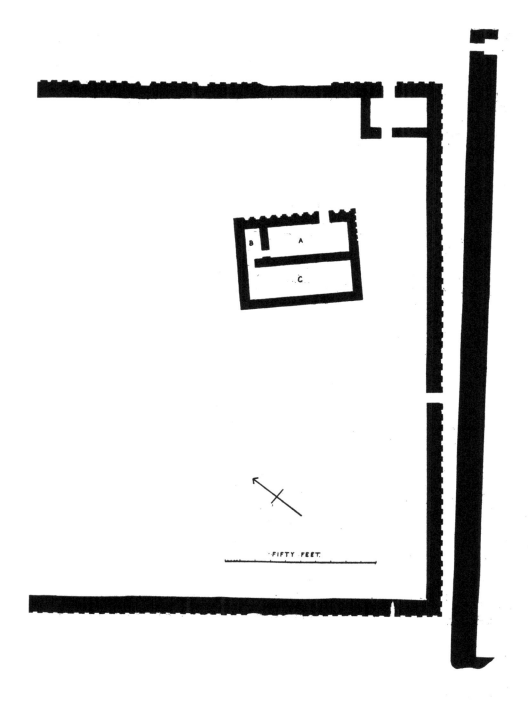

FIFTY FEET.

E.R.A.

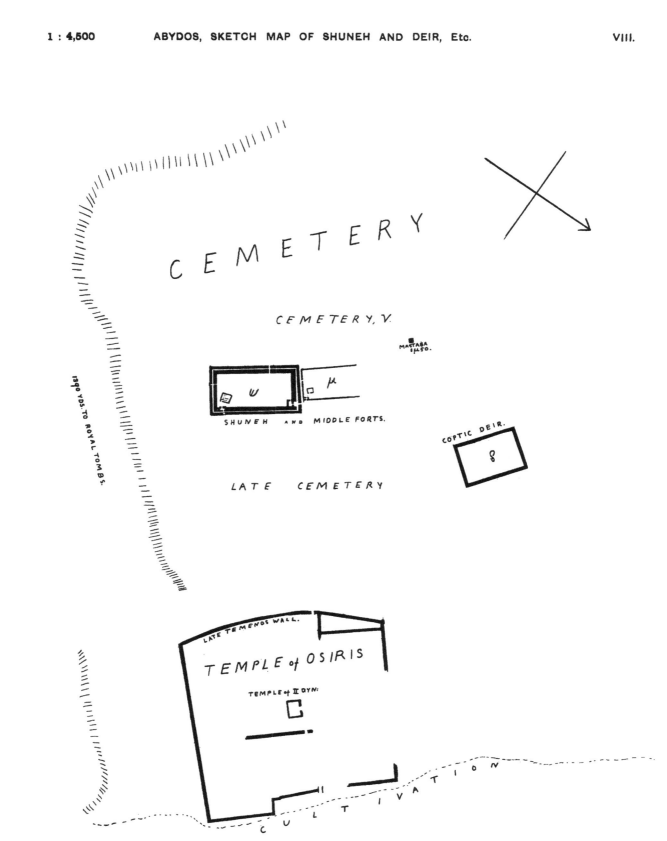

CEMETERY

CEMETERY, V.

MASTABA
§ μ 50.

SHUNEH   AND   MIDDLE FORTS.

COPTIC DEIR.

LATE   CEMETERY

1390 YDS. TO ROYAL TOMBS.

LATE TEMENOS WALL.

TEMPLE of OSIRIS

TEMPLE of II DYN:

CULTIVATION

E.R.A.

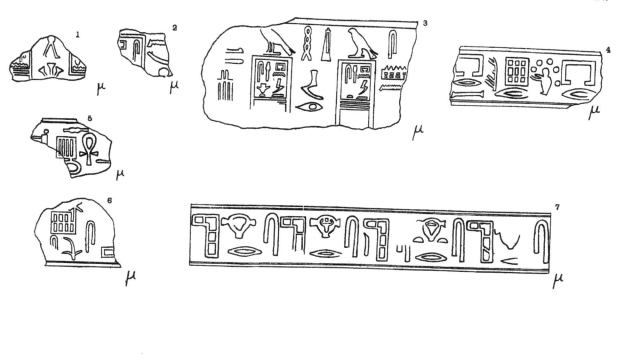

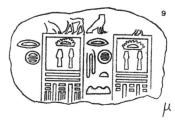

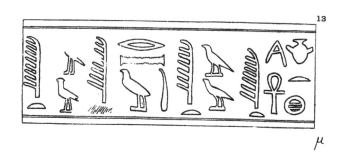

F. H.
E. R. A.

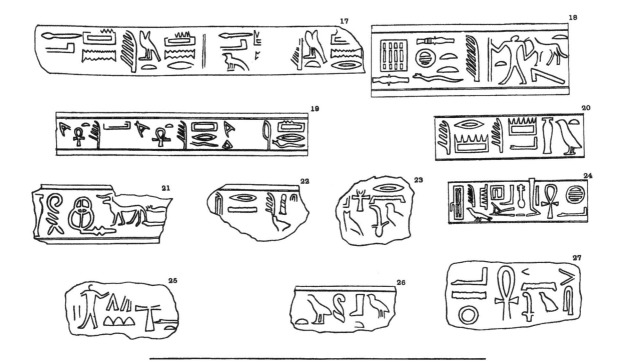

MARKS INCISED ON MUD SEALINGS.

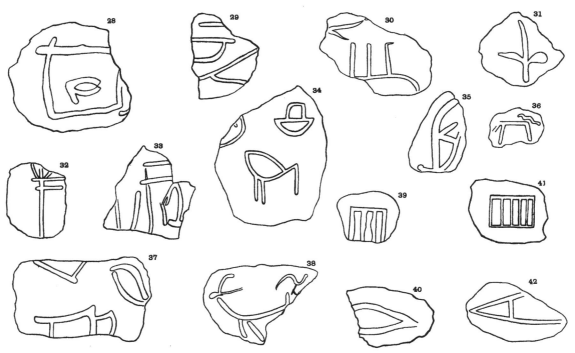

F. H.
E.R.A.

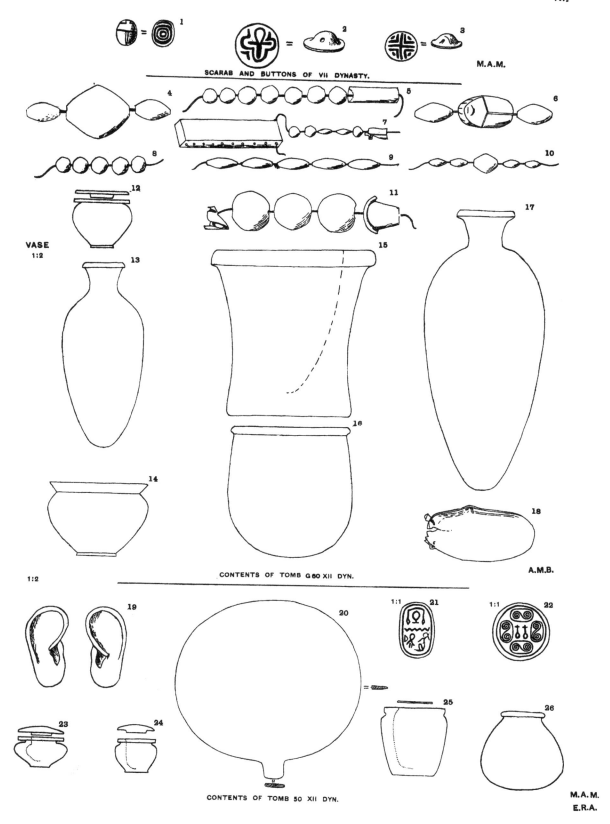

SCARAB AND BUTTONS OF VII DYNASTY.

M.A.M.

VASE
1:2

CONTENTS OF TOMB G 60 XII DYN.

A.M.B.

1:2

CONTENTS OF TOMB 50 XII DYN.

M.A.M.
E.R.A.

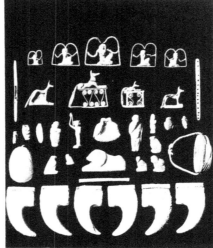

1. SELECTED JEWELLRY FROM V. 21.   2. JEWELLRY FROM TOMB V. 21.   3. STELE OF AY.

4 & 5. COLOSSAL GRANITE HEAD FROM OSIRIS TEMPLE.

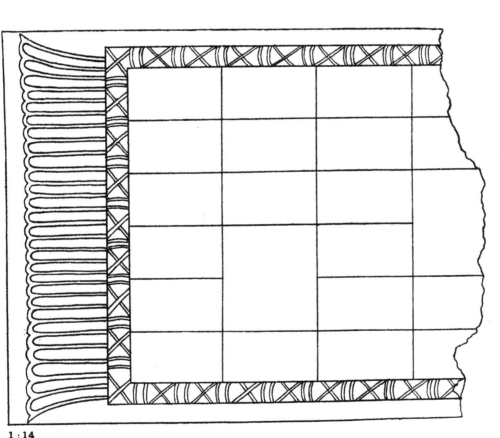

1:14

SKETCH OF STELE.

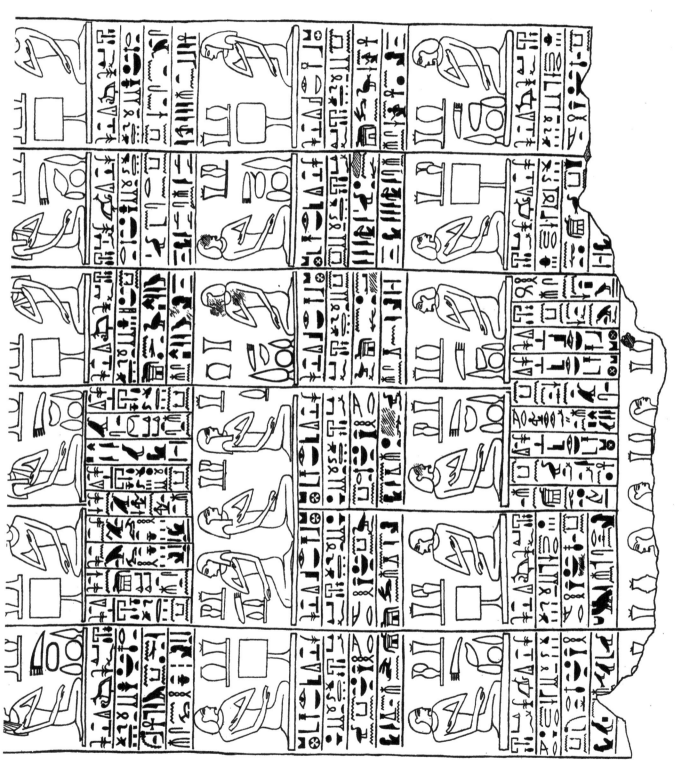

A.E.P.W.

F.H.

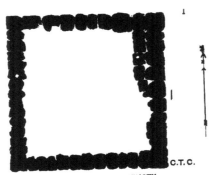

TOMB CHAPEL OF AY XII DYNASTY.

1 : 1

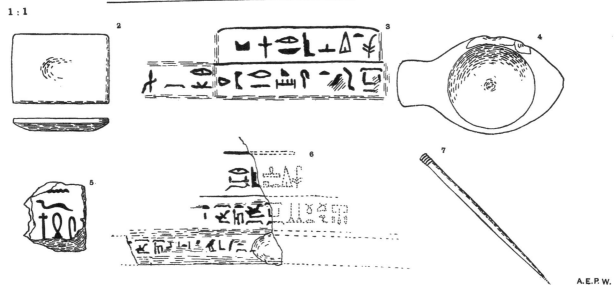

MISCELLANEOUS OBJECTS. XII—XVIII DYN.

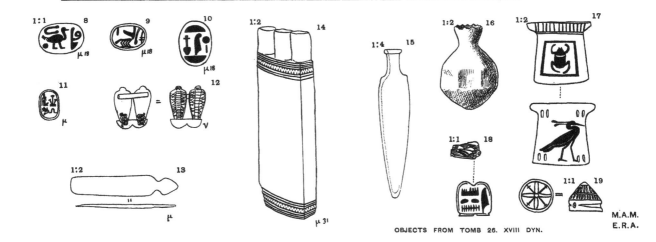

OBJECTS FROM TOMB 26. XVIII DYN.

1. IVORY HANDLE OF TRAY.　　2. IVORY KOHL POT. (μ 31)　　3. FOREIGN FIGURE AND EGYPTIAN VASE. (ω 1.)

4　　　　RING VASE AND FIGURE VASE.—GRAECO-EGYPTIAN.　　　　5.

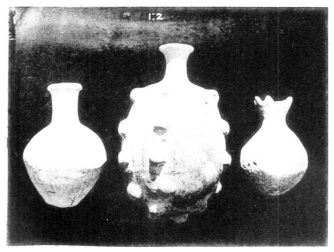

6. VASES FROM V 15. V 24. μ 26　　　　7. OBJECTS FROM TOMB. μ 26

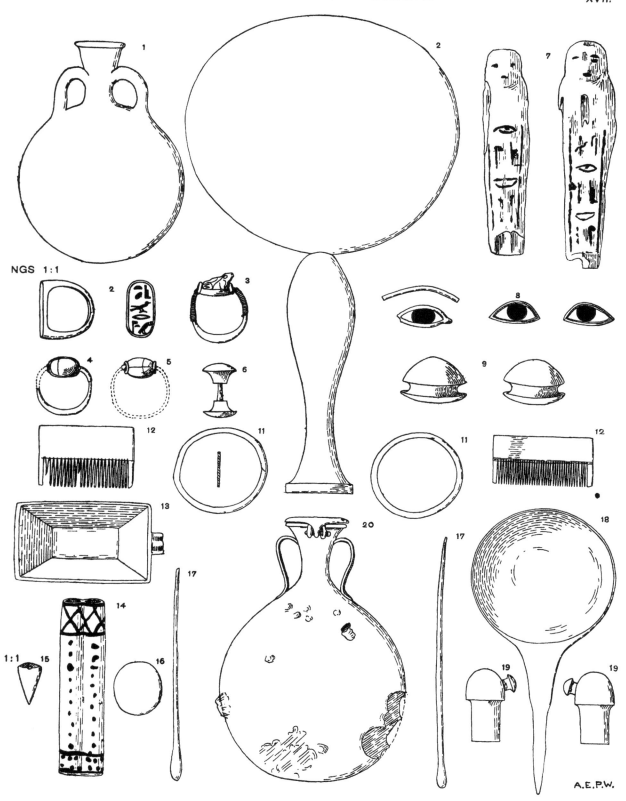

NGS 1:1

1:1

A.E.P.W.

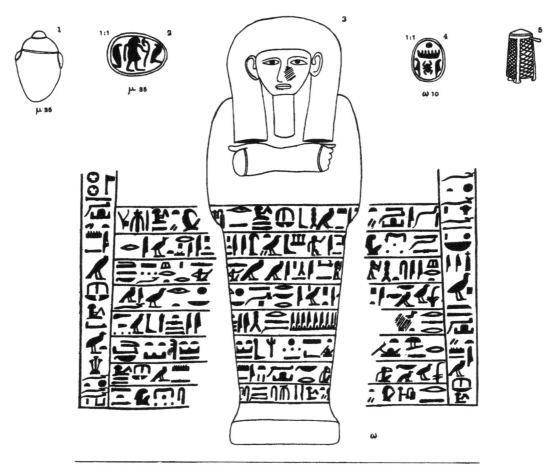

CONTENTS OF TOMB μ 36

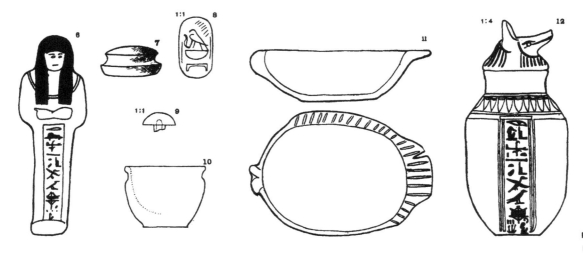

M.A.M.
E.R.A.

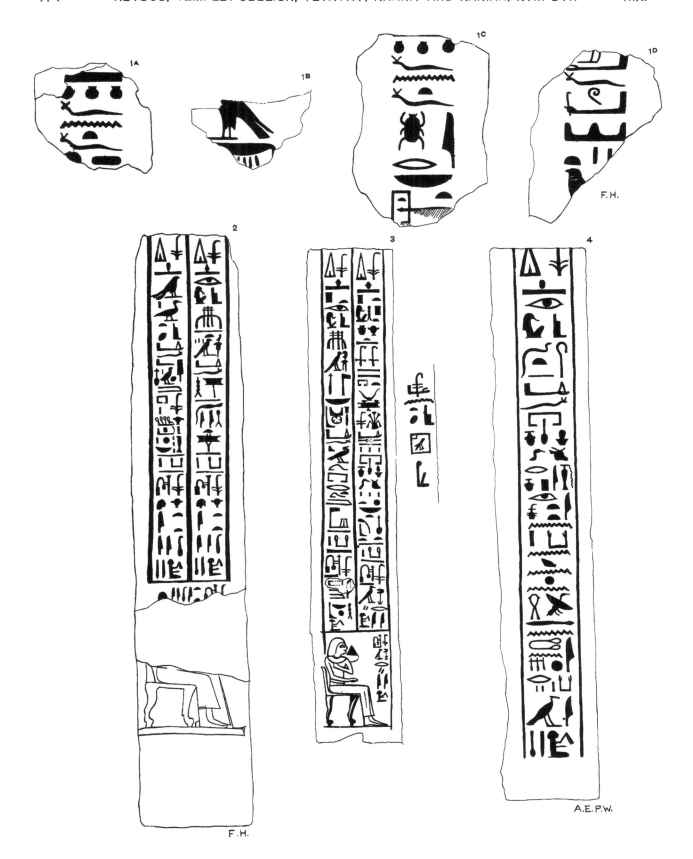

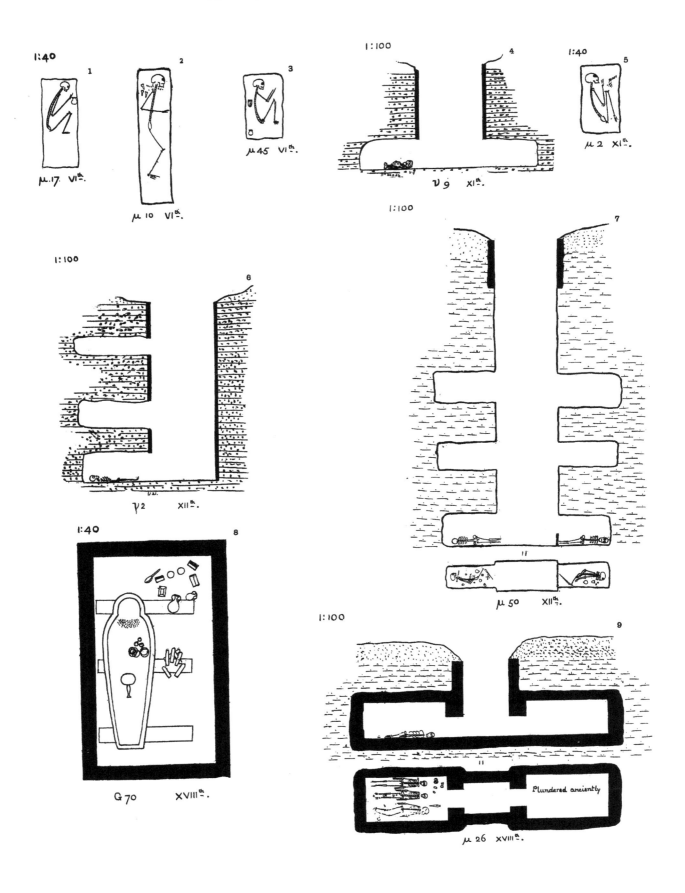

1:40

1

μ.17. VIᵗʰ.

2

μ 10 VIᵗʰ.

3

μ 45 VIᵗʰ.

1:100

4

ν 9 XIᵗʰ.

1:40

5

μ 2 XIᵗʰ.

1:100

6

ν 2 XIIᵗʰ.

1:100

7

11

μ 50 XIIᵗʰ.

1:40

8

G 70 XVIIIᵗʰ.

1:100

9

11

Plundered anciently

μ 26 XVIIIᵗʰ.

1. SLAB OF AAHMES I. FROM OSIRIS TEMPLE.

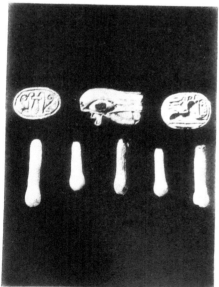

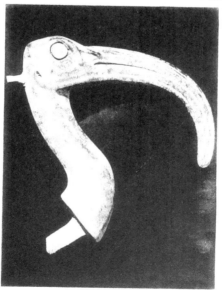

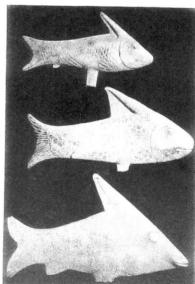

2. OBJECTS FROM CEMETERY.   3. (1 : 3) BRONZE IBIS HEAD FROM SHUNEH.   4. (1 : 2) BRONZE FISHES FROM SHUNEH.

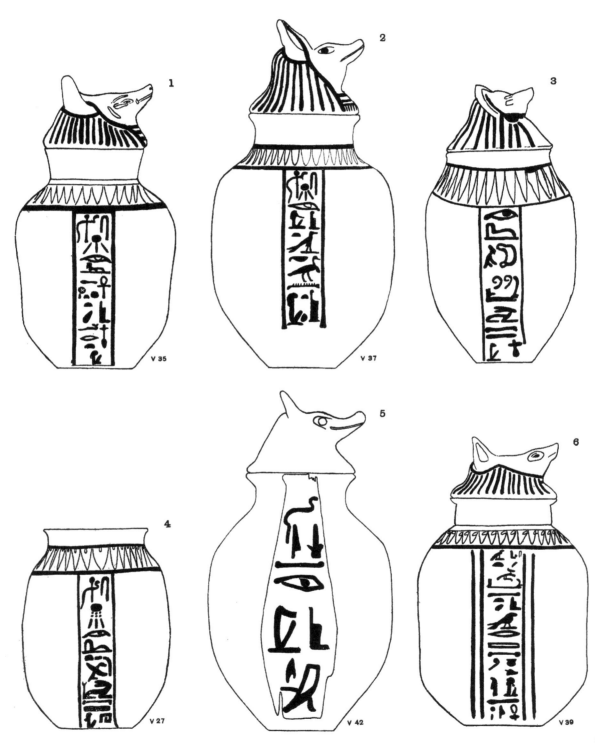

E.R.A.
C.T.C.

1. TYPES OF USHABTIS FOUND IN THE POTS.

2. USHABTI POT AND USHABTIS.

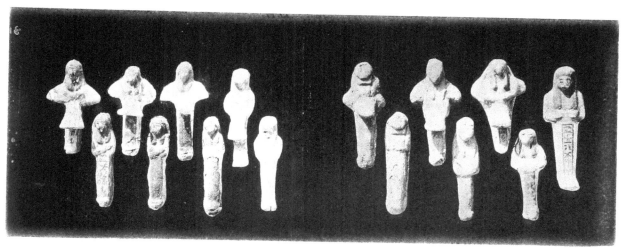

3. TYPICAL USHABTIS FOUND IN THE POTS

4. TYPES OF POTTERY FROM THE IBIS CEMETERY.

5. INFANT'S COFFIN.

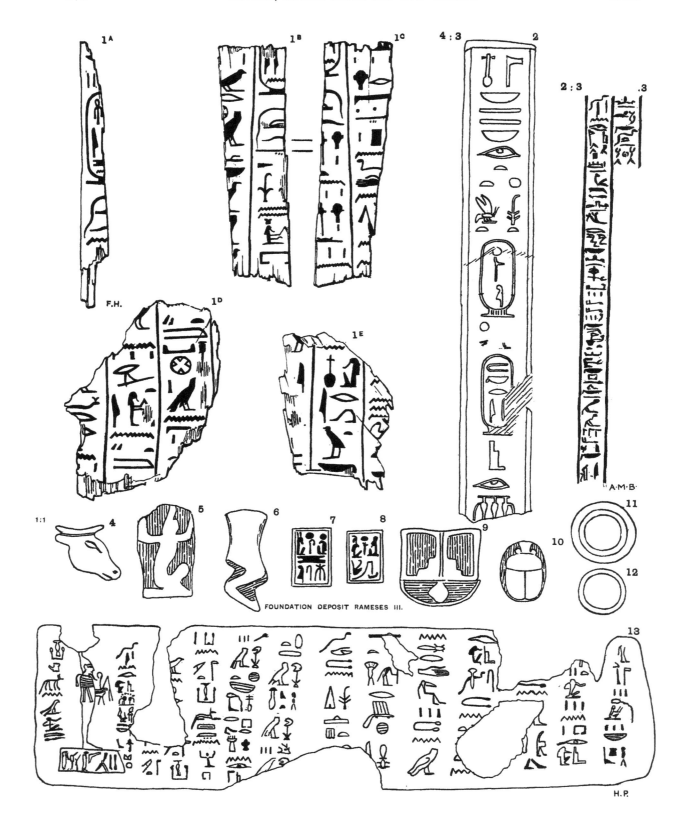

FOUNDATION DEPOSIT RAMESES III.

1:3

1:7

F.H.

H.P.

M.A.M.
F.H.

East Wall.

East Wall.

North Wall.

West Wall.

East Wall

M. A.M.

1. TOMB OF HOR-DEDU-ANKH.

2. HEAD OF PSAMTEK (?)

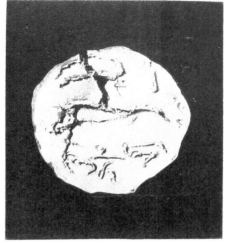

3. MUD SEALING FROM SHUNEH.

4. BUST OF NEKHT HORHEB. (See AB. I. LXX. 12)

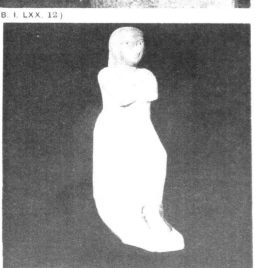

5. INFANTS' COFFINS FROM SHUNEH. 6, 7. GILDED STATUETTE FROM SHUNEH.

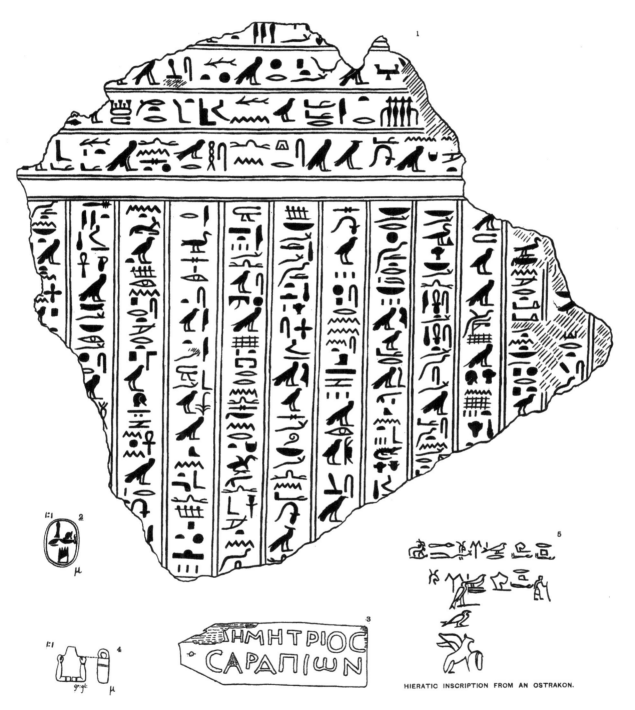

HIERATIC INSCRIPTION FROM AN OSTRAKON.

M.A.M.

F.H.

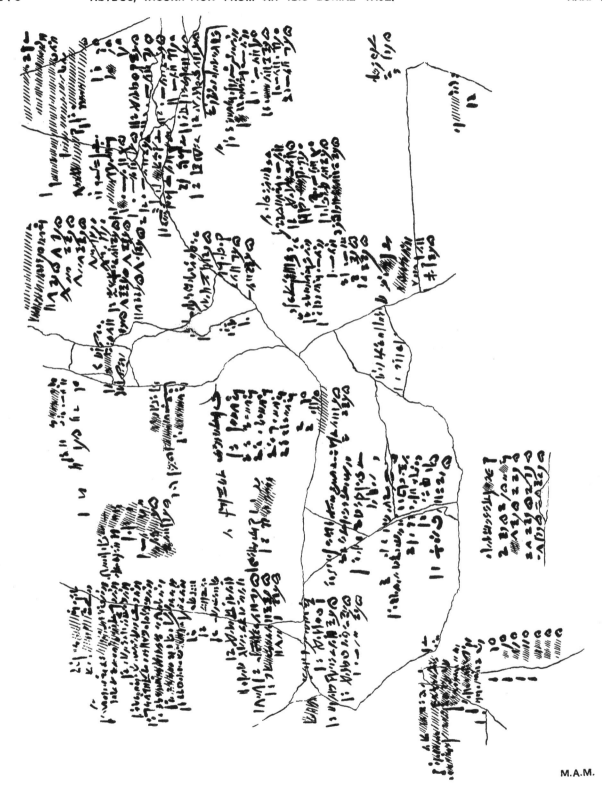

M.A.M.

SLATE.

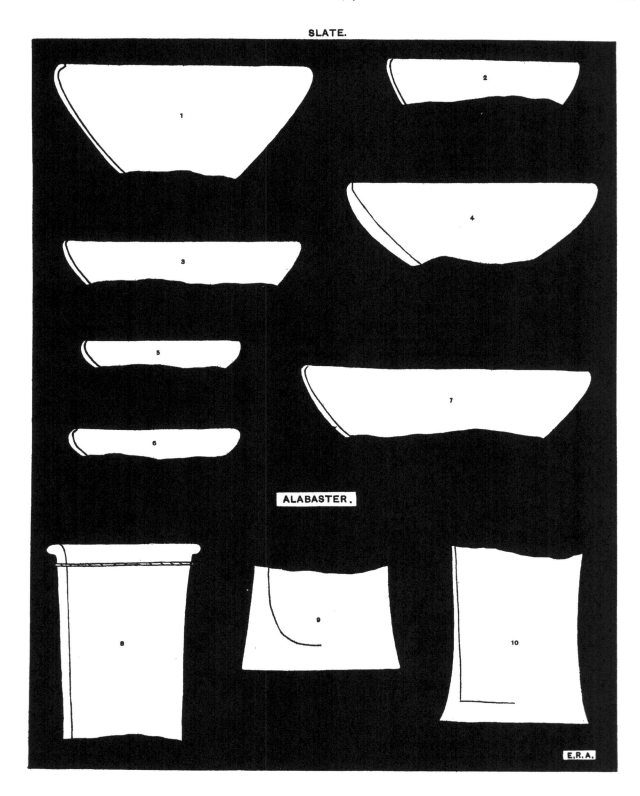

ALABASTER.

E.R.A.

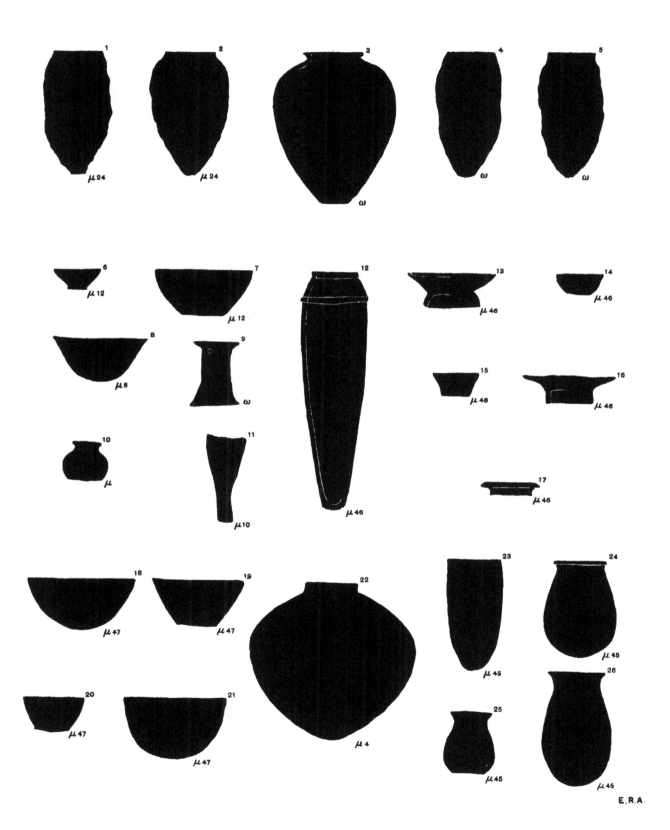

E.R.A.

XI   XII

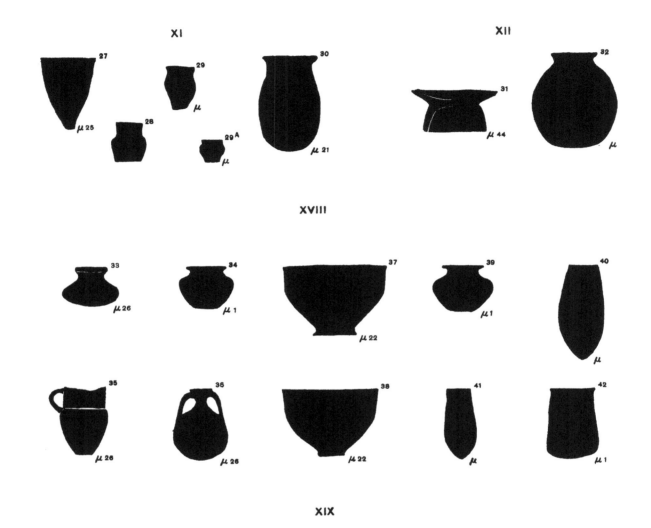

XVIII

XIX

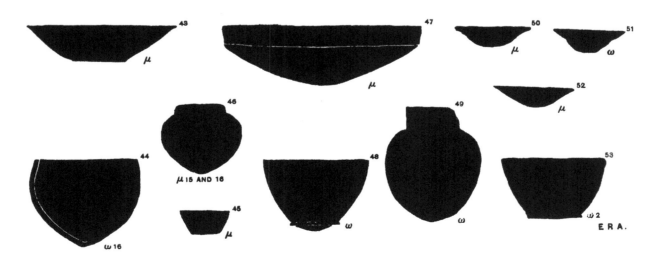

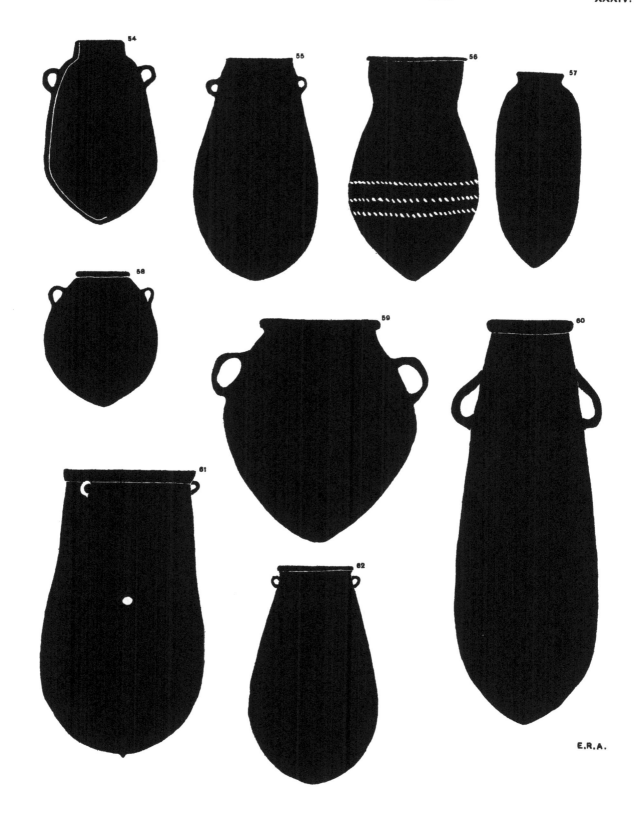

E.R.A.

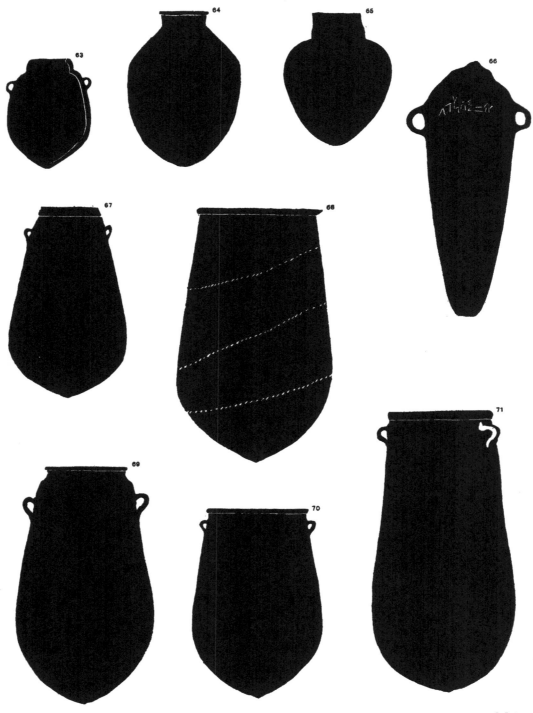

E.R.A.

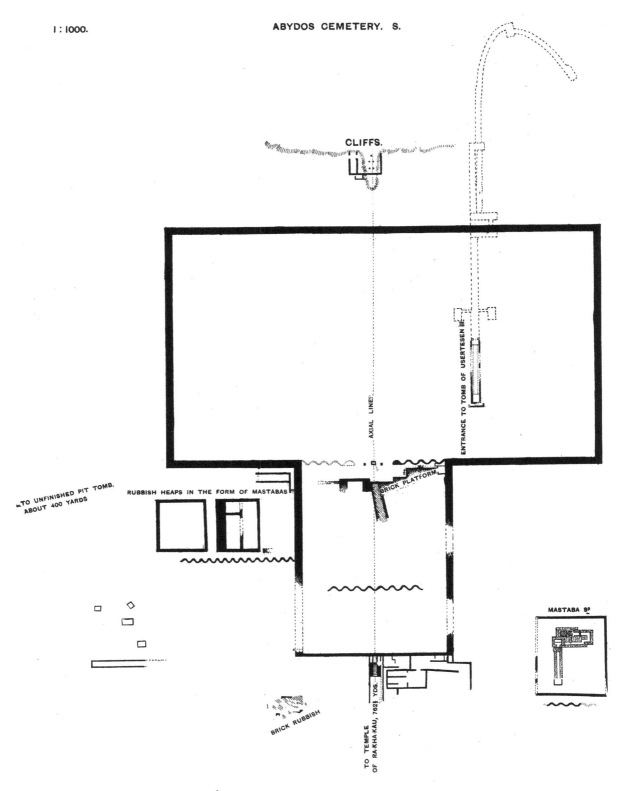

1 : 1000.

ABYDOS CEMETERY. S.

CLIFFS.

AXIAL LINE.

ENTRANCE TO TOMB OF USERTESEN III.

TO UNFINISHED PIT TOMB, ABOUT 400 YARDS

RUBBISH HEAPS IN THE FORM OF MASTABAS

BRICK PLATFORM

MASTABA 99

BRICK RUBBISH

TO TEMPLE OF RA.KHA.KAU, 762½ YDS.

GENERAL PLÀN OF THE COURTYARD OF THE TOMB OF USERTESEN III.
AND SURROUNDING BUILDINGS.

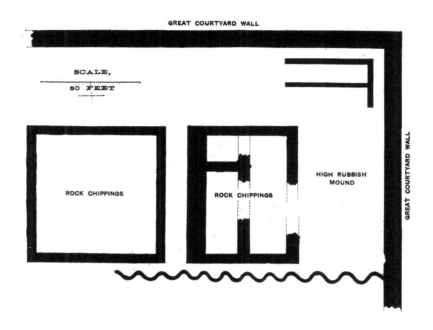

GREAT COURTYARD WALL

SCALE,

50 FEET

ROCK CHIPPINGS

ROCK CHIPPINGS

HIGH RUBBISH MOUND

GREAT COURTYARD WALL

DUMMY MASTABAS COVERING ROCK CHIPPINGS FROM TOMB OF USERTESEN III.

1 : 200

MASTABA S¹⁰

BRICK PLATFORM

TOMBS S².

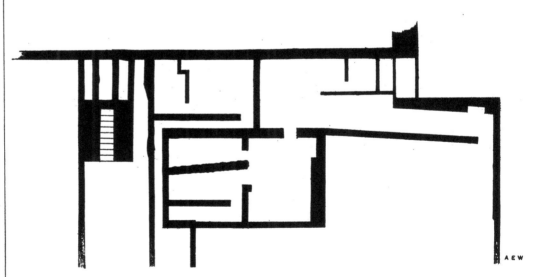

A E W

CHAMBERS AND STAIRWAY AT ENTRANCE OF GREAT COURTYARD

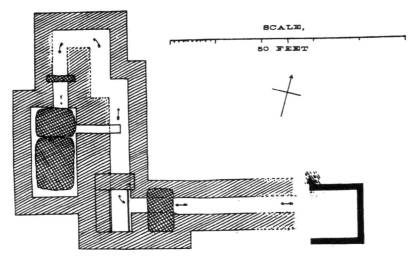

SCALE,

50 FEET

MASTABA S⁹

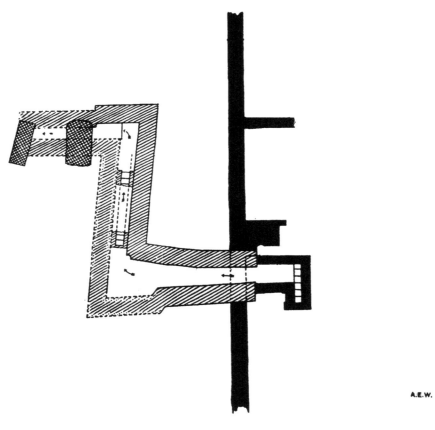

A.E.W.

MASTABA S¹⁰

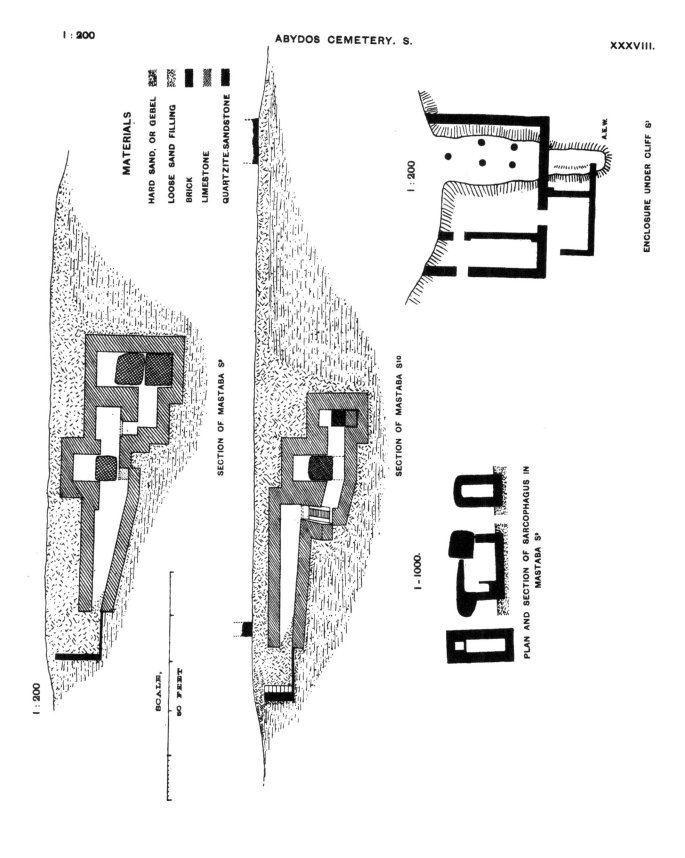

1 : 200

MATERIALS

HARD SAND, OR GEBEL
LOOSE SAND FILLING
BRICK
LIMESTONE
QUARTZITE-SANDSTONE

SECTION OF MASTABA S⁹

SCALE,
50 FEET

SECTION OF MASTABA S¹⁰

1 : 200

ENCLOSURE UNDER CLIFF S¹

A.E.W.

1 - 1000.

PLAN AND SECTION OF SARCOPHAGUS IN
MASTABA S⁹

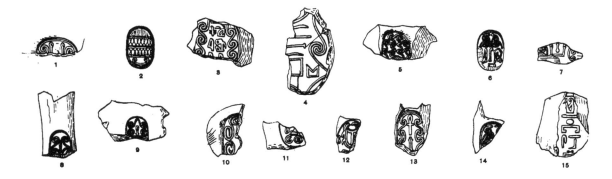

1 : 6

CLAY SCARAB SEALINGS FROM DUMMY MASTABA, S⁸

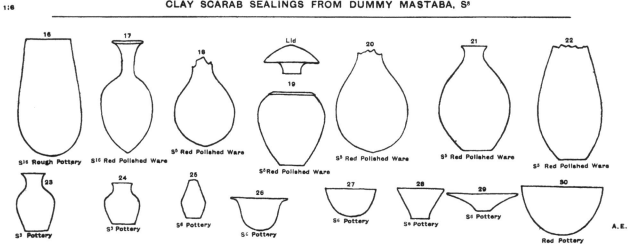

A.E.

POTTERY FROM FOUNDATION DEPOSITS etc.

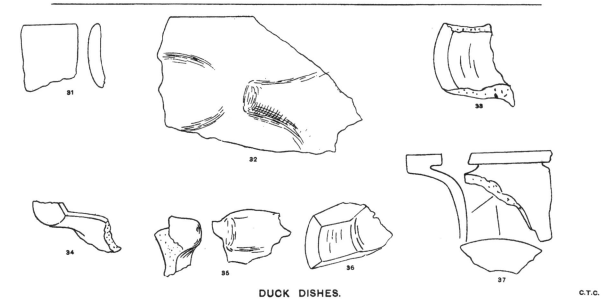

DUCK DISHES.

C.T.C.

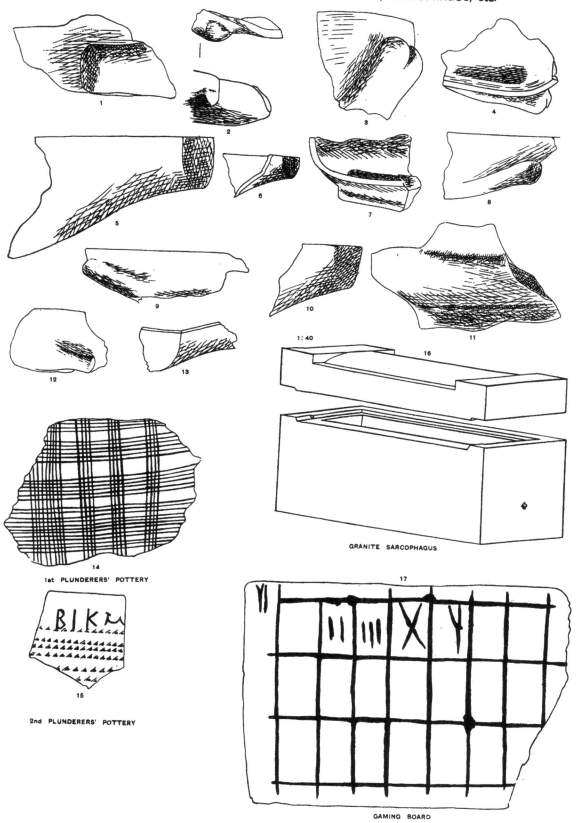

1st PLUNDERERS' POTTERY

2nd PLUNDERERS' POTTERY

GRANITE SARCOPHAGUS

GAMING BOARD

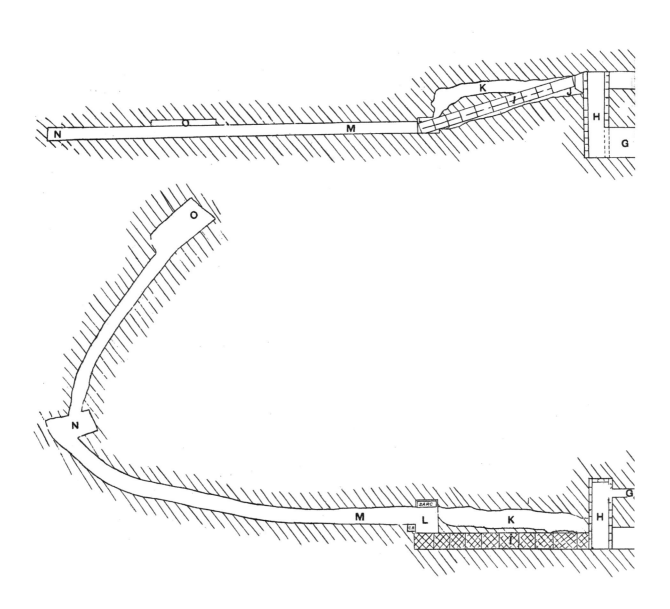

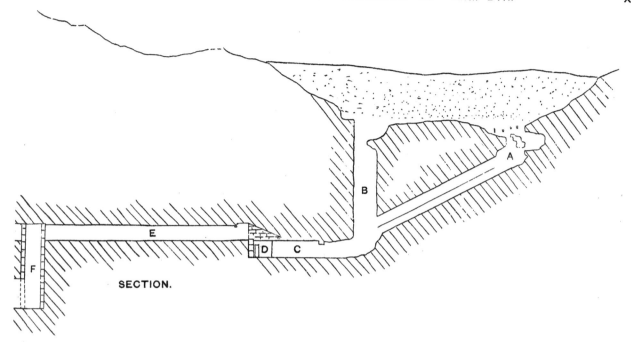

SECTION.

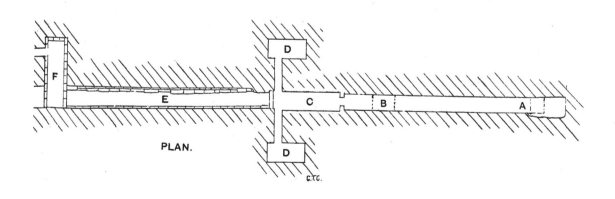

PLAN.

c.t.c.

1. GENERAL VIEW.

2. ASCENT TO TEMENOS.

3. ASCENT TO TEMENOS.

4. WAVY WALL ACROSS TEMENOS.

5. WAVY WALL SCREENING THE DUMMY MASTABA.

6. METHOD OF CLEARING THE STRAIGHT SHAFT.

7. THE WORKMEN'S STAIRS.

8 NORTH WALL OF TEMENOS.

1. POLE ROOF. CHAMBER C.

2. GRANITE BLOCK FALLEN INTO ROOM H.

3. VIEW OF THE AAHMES TOWN. AAHMES PYRAMID IN THE DISTANCE.

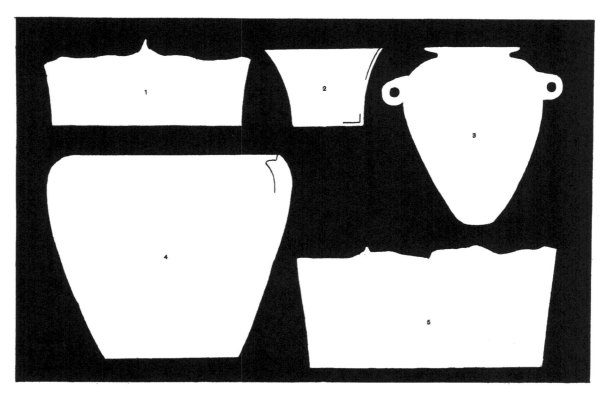

ABYDOS: TOWN OF AAHMES I.   STONE BOWLS.

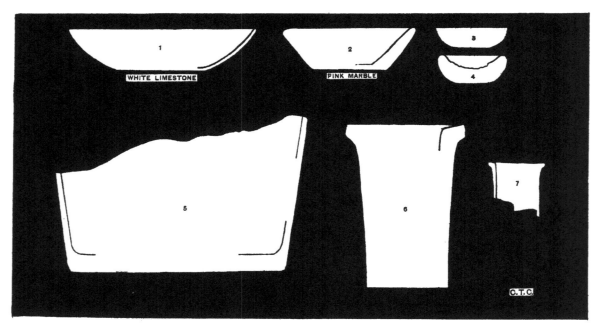

1. SOUTH ENTRANCE GATE AND STEPS

2. FRONT BRICK RETAINING WALL. ABADI BOY.

3. THE CORNER DEPOSIT.

4. THE NORTH END OF TEMPLE.
2nd STONE RETAINING WALL.

5. LOOKING NORTH, SLOPING ASCENT IN FOREGROUND,
MEN STANDING ON THE FIRST TERRACE.

2 : 3

ABYDOS: TERRACE TEMPLE FOUNDATION DEPOSIT XVIIIth DYN.
ALABASTER AND PAINTED LIMESTONE.

XLVI.

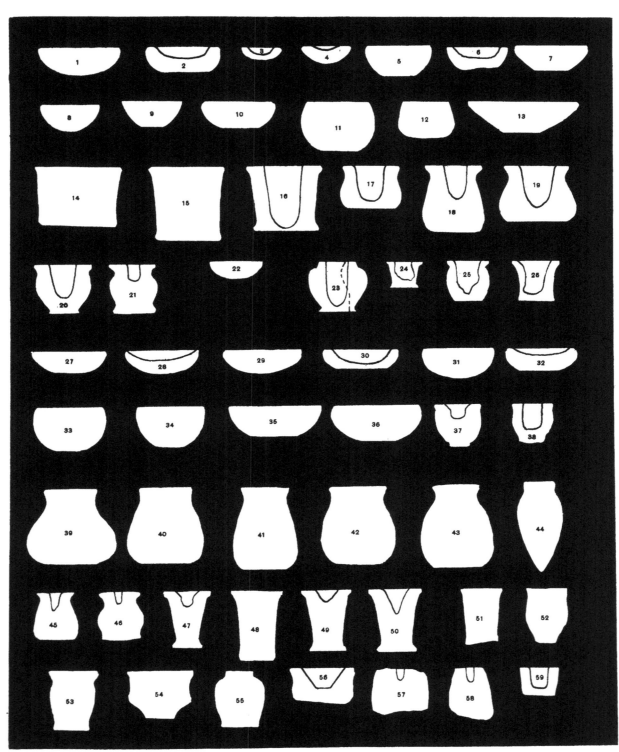

C.T.C.

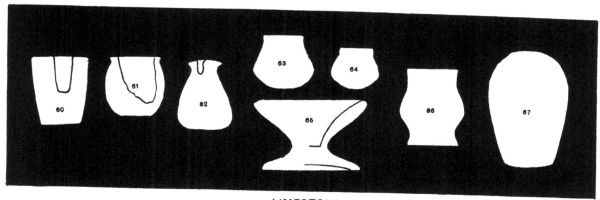

LIMESTONE

1:3

POTTERY.

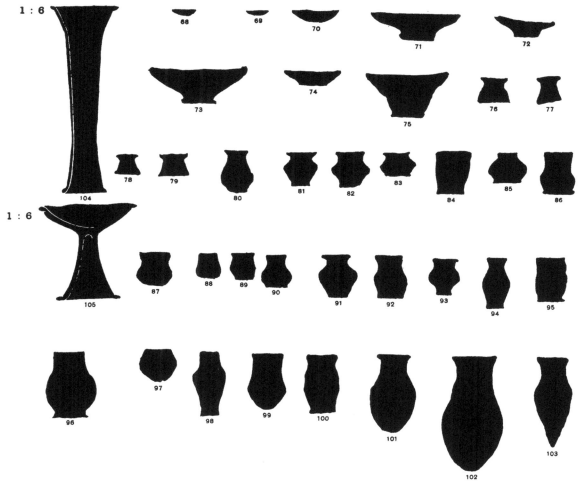

C.T.C.

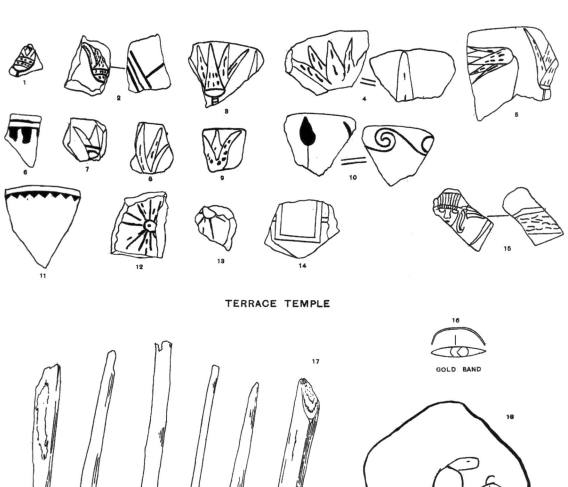

TERRACE TEMPLE

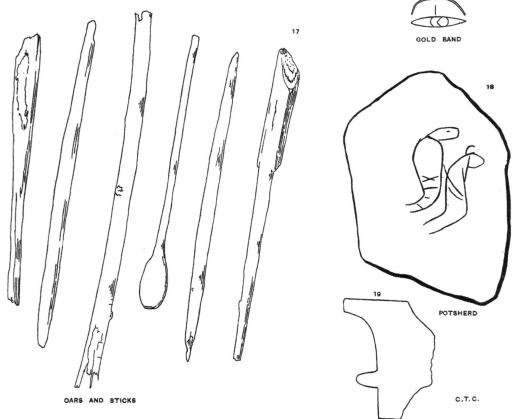

OARS AND STICKS

GOLD BAND

POTSHERD

PIECE OF CORNICE

C.T.C.

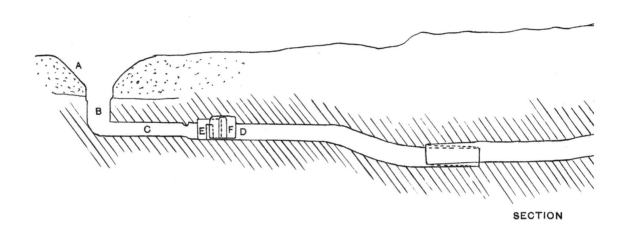

SECTION

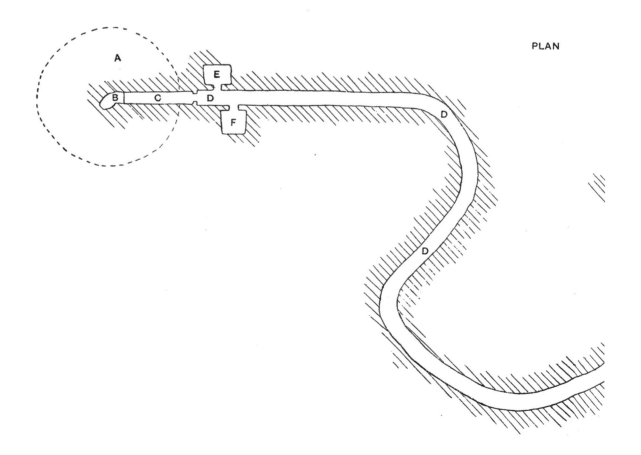

PLAN

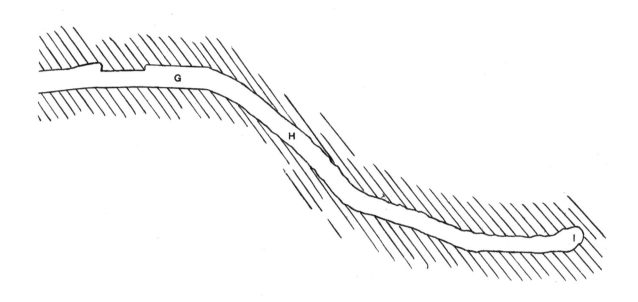

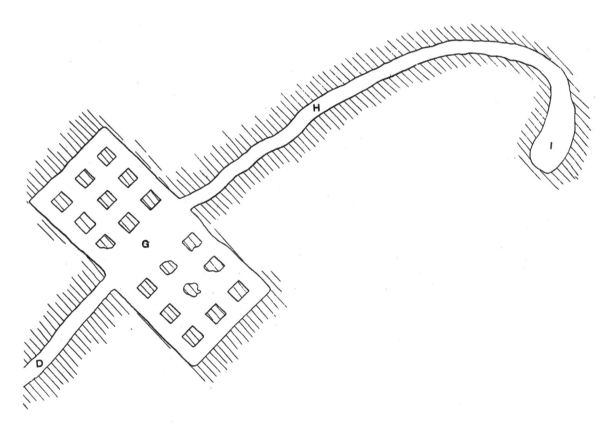

O.T.C.

1. STELE OF QUEEN TETA SHERA.　　2. STELE OF QUEEN TETA SHERA.

3 4 & 5. FIGURES FROM THE CEMETERY, SHRINE AND TOWN.

6 & 7. USHABTI FIGURES FROM AAHMES CEMETERY.　8. ENTRANCE TO TOMB OF AAHMES I.

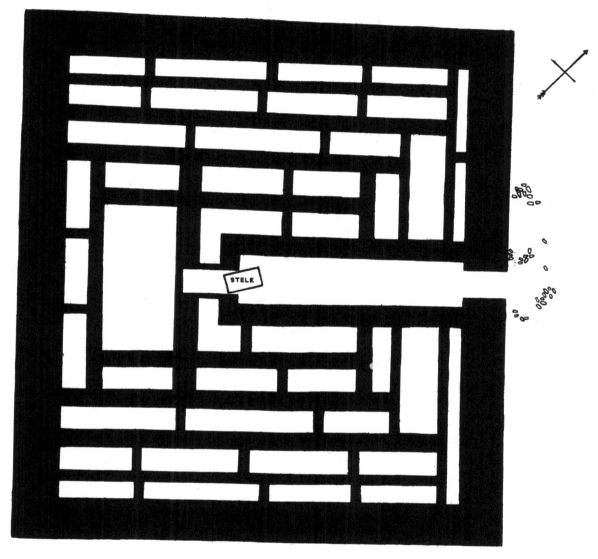

STELE

C.T.C.

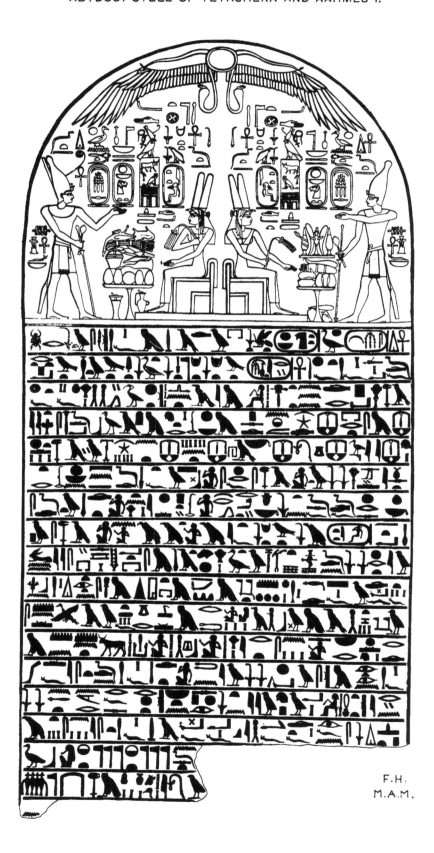

F.H.
M.A.M.

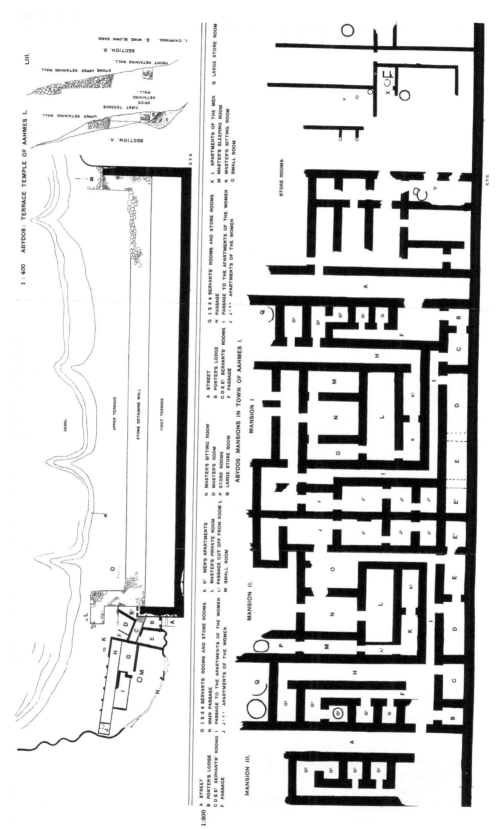

The material originally positioned here is too large for reproduction in this reissue. A PDF can be downloaded from the web address given on page iv of this book, by clicking on 'Resources Available'.

Facs. WSp.

Facs. WSp.

I Recto.

I Verso

II

1. BEFORE STARTING THE WORK.

2. STREET H OF HOUSE 1, LOOKING EAST.

3. STREET H OF HOUSE 1, LOOKING WEST.

4. WALLS IN HOUSE 2.

5. STORE CHAMBERS, POT AND SQUARE BIN X.

6. STORE ROOMS Y.

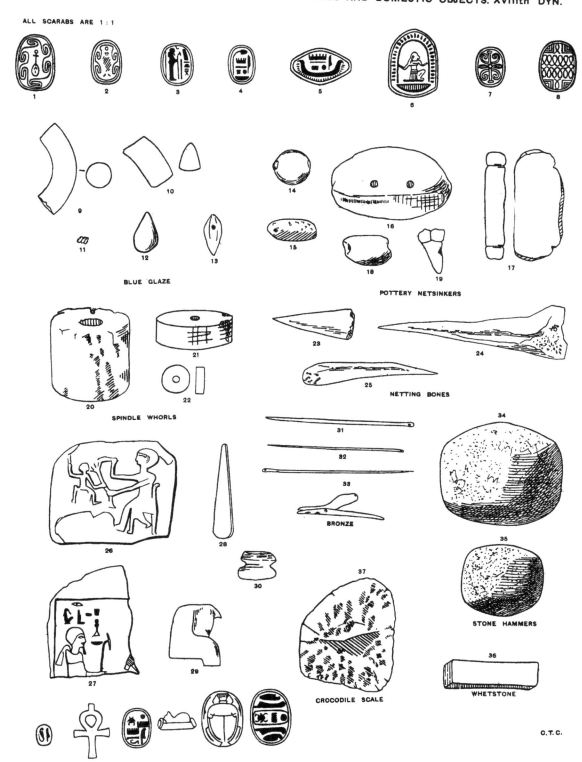

ALL SCARABS ARE 1 : 1

BLUE GLAZE

POTTERY NETSINKERS

SPINDLE WHORLS

NETTING BONES

BRONZE

STONE HAMMERS

WHETSTONE

CROCODILE SCALE

C.T.C.

FROM A TOMB IN THE AAHMES CEMETERY.

BLACK INCISED POTTERY

XIIth DYN. STYLES CONTINUED TO XVIIIth DYN.

11. SPOUT OF FALSE NECKED VASE.   8,9,10, IMPORTED MEDITERRANEAN POTTERY

IVORY

BRONZE

LIMESTONE KOHL POT

CLAY TOYS

C.T.C.

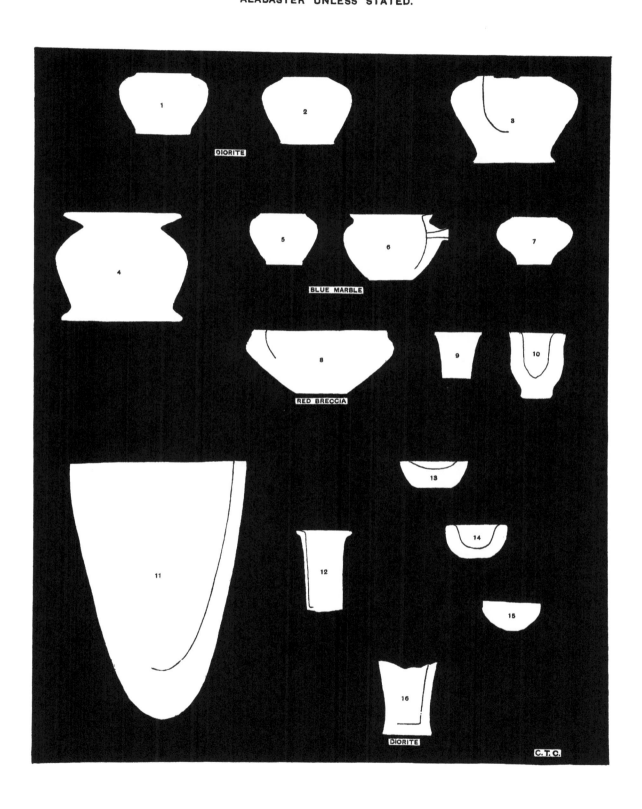

F. H.

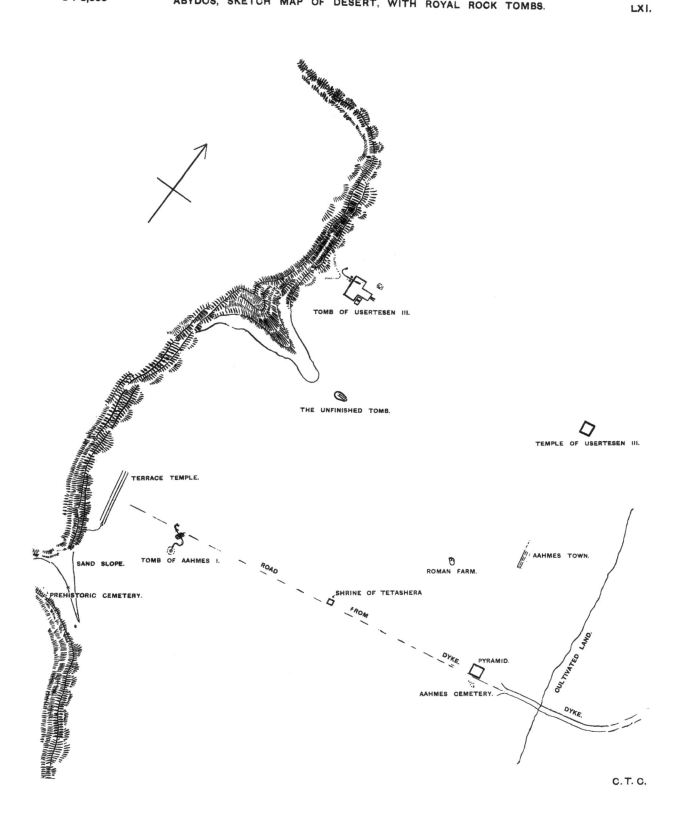

TOMB OF USERTESEN III.

THE UNFINISHED TOMB.

TEMPLE OF USERTESEN III.

TERRACE TEMPLE.

SAND SLOPE.   TOMB OF AAHMES I.   ROAD   ROMAN FARM.   AAHMES TOWN.

PREHISTORIC CEMETERY.

SHRINE OF TETASHERA

FROM

CULTIVATED LAND.

DYKE.   PYRAMID.

AAHMES CEMETERY.

DYKE.

C. T. C.

For EU product safety concerns, contact us at Calle de José Abascal, 56–1°,
28003 Madrid, Spain or eugpsr@cambridge.org.

www.ingramcontent.com/pod-product-compliance
Ingram Content Group UK Ltd.
Pitfield, Milton Keynes, MK11 3LW, UK
UKHW051029150625

459647UK00023B/2865